C000246368

Introducing God's Plan

Sylvia and Michael Penny

ISBN: 978-1-78364-370-7

2018: Second Edition

The Open Bible Trust
Fordland Mount, Upper Basildon,
Reading, RG8 8LU, UK.

www.obt.org.uk

**"See, I have engraved you
on the palms of my hands."
(Isaiah 49:16)**

There is a series of free YouTube videos of
Sylvia Penny reading the text of this book.
Also, there are two audio CDs available of her reading the text
and details of these can be seen on www.obt.org.uk

∎∎

Contents

Page

Ways of using this book

This book can be used in a number of ways. Parents can read it to their children. Adults and older children can read it themselves. There is an audio book of *Introducing God's Plan* on two Cs available from the Open Bible Trust (www.obt.org.uk) and children can simply listen to the CDs or they can follow the words in the book while listening to the audio book.

At the end of each chapter there are some questions. Parents can ask children these questions. Adults or older children may care to answer them themselves.

Following the questions is a list of the main Bible references on which the chapter has been based. Adults may care to look up these references and read them. They can be read at the end of each chapter of this book. However, at the end of the book, see *Appendix 3 – Readings from the Bible*, all of these readings are collected together, with other readings which impinge on the subject matter. Thus a person may prefer to read right through this book, and then read through those Bible readings.

Sometimes extra information is given just before the last page of each chapter, which is a summary of God's plan up to the end of the chapter just read.

In the text of the book there are some references to end-notes which deal in more depth with a particular point.

All of the material in this book has been tried and tested by various people from the ages of seven to seventy. We are most grateful to them all and thank them for their diligence. Their comments and criticisms, their suggestions and ideas, have enabled us to improve this book considerably.

We pray that He will bless this work which seeks to glorify Him and His plan for mankind which is centred in Jesus Christ, our Saviour and Lord.

1. Adam and Eve in the Garden of Eden

(Genesis 1-3)

A long time ago there was God. He was all alone, and there was nothing else besides Him. There were no stars, no moon and no sun. There was no heaven and no earth.

So God made these things for Himself. First, He made the heavens and the earth and He also made many angels to live in heaven. After a while one of these angels became jealous of God, and all that God could do. In fact, he wanted to be God himself and because of this he was always trying to spoil the good things which God had done. This angel's name was Satan.

Then God made light, which He separated from the darkness, and that was the first day.

On the second day God separated the water so that some was above the sky and some was below it.

On the third day God gathered the waters on the earth together and called it the sea. The earth that appeared became dry ground, which He called land. He also made the land produce plants of all sorts - trees and bushes, flowers and shrubs. He made every kind that produces seeds and nuts, fruits and vegetables.

On the fourth day God put lights in the sky - the sun, the moon and the stars. On the fifth day God made all the fish and other creatures that live in water, and He also made all the birds which fly above the earth.

On the sixth day God made all the animals which live on the land, and He saw that everything He had made was good.

Then God made man in His own image. He said that man should rule over all the living things He had created - the fish and the birds and the animals. He also said that all the plants He had made were there to be food for man and all the living creatures. God said that everything He had made was very good, and that was the end of the sixth day.

By the seventh day God had finished all His work. The world was complete.

The two trees

The man whom God had made was called Adam. God created Adam as a perfect man, and so at the beginning, Adam never did anything wrong. However, God also gave Adam the ability to choose what he would do. As long as Adam chose to obey God, he would remain perfect and never die.

God had made a garden in Eden, as part of His creation, and it was in this garden that God placed Adam. In the middle of the garden were two special trees. One was "the tree of life", and one was "the tree of the knowledge of good and evil". God put Adam in the Garden of Eden to take care of it. He told Adam that he could eat the fruit from any of the trees in the garden except the tree of the knowledge of good and evil. If he ate from that tree, God told him he would die.

Then God brought to Adam all the animals and birds which He had created, to see what names Adam would give them. But none of these were suitable to help Adam, and God said that it was not good for Adam to remain alone. So God made a woman, and brought her to Adam to help him, and to become his wife.

Adam named his wife Eve, because she was to become the mother of everyone who would ever live on earth. So Adam and Eve were very happy together in the Garden of Eden. Adam told Eve everything God had said to him, and so she knew that she must not eat the fruit from "the tree of the knowledge of good and evil".

Satan and the fruit

However, one day Satan, the wicked angel who was jealous of God, came to Eve in the garden. He told her to eat the fruit from "the tree of the knowledge of good and evil", but Eve refused at first. She remembered what God had said and she wanted to obey Him. She told Satan that God had said she would die if she ate the fruit.

Satan called God a liar. He told Eve she would not die if she ate the fruit. Instead she would become like God, knowing good and evil. So Eve looked at the fruit, and saw that it looked good to eat. She took some and ate it, and gave some of the fruit to Adam and he ate it as well.

When Adam and Eve had eaten the fruit they heard God walking in the garden and they were afraid. Adam and Eve knew that they had done wrong. They tried to hide from God, but when God called out to Adam, and asked where he was, they could hide no longer.

God looked at them and asked Adam if they had eaten the fruit from "the tree of the knowledge of good and evil". Adam told God that Eve had given him some of the fruit to eat, so God turned to Eve and asked her why she had disobeyed Him. Eve told God that Satan had persuaded her to eat the fruit, because he had said that she would not die if she ate it.

Then God was very angry with Satan because of what he had done, and the lies he had told Eve. God told Satan that one day he would also die[1].

Things change

Everything was no longer perfect, including Adam and Eve. They had disobeyed God and slowly their bodies began to wear out. Now they were going to grow old and die.

The ground was also changed and God told Adam that now he would have to work hard to grow food to eat. Adam would have to dig the ground, weed it, and make it ready for plants. Before, when everything had been perfect, the plants had grown without any work.

God then sent Adam and Eve out of the garden and set up a guard to make sure they would never be able to get back in again. This was because God did not want Adam and Eve to eat the fruit of "the tree of life". If they did this they would live forever as disobedient people, but Adam and Eve were to die as God had said.

They were no longer happy all the time, and sometimes they thought of how lovely everything had been in the garden. They were very sad, and very sorry for what they had done, and how it had spoiled everything around them.

****

The Fertile Crescent

This is where people think life began, and where the Garden of Eden may have been situated.

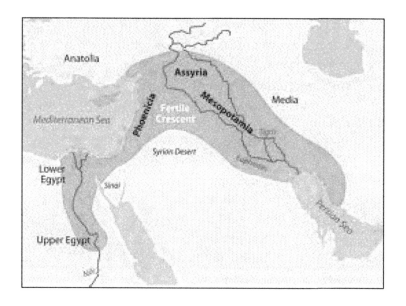

Adam and Eve in the Garden of Eden

Questions

1. What is the name of the first angel who sinned?
2. What was his sin?
3. What are the names of the first people who sinned?
4. What was their sin?
5. What was the result of their first sin?

Main references

Job	38:4-7	Angels witnessed God creating
Ezekiel	28:11-19	Satan's pride and wickedness
Genesis	1:26; 2:7	Adam is created
	2:21-22	Eve is created
	3:1	Satan tempts Eve
	3:15	Satan will one day die
	3:17-19	The ground is cursed
	3:23-24	Adam and Eve sent out of the garden

Please read now, or after you have read this book:

Genesis 1 & 2; Ezekiel 28:11-19; Genesis 3.

God's Plan so far

God
Heaven - and all the angels
Satan
Earth - and all animals
Adam and Eve

2. Noah and the Flood

(Genesis 4-9)

Adam and Eve had been shut out of the beautiful Garden of Eden. They had disobeyed God and now they had to work hard to grow themselves food to eat and make clothes to wear.

Over the years, Adam and Eve had a number of children - both boys and girls. Their first two sons were called Cain and Abel. Cain and Abel had to work hard to help their mother and father. Abel looked after the sheep which roamed over the hills and valleys near where they lived. Cain helped to dig the ground, taking out the weeds and making it ready to grow the plants they needed for food.

Adam and Eve told Cain and Abel and their other children how sad and sorry they were that they had disobeyed God in the garden of Eden. Abel wanted to obey God and do what God wanted him to do. Abel was a good man and pleased God because he was obedient. He brought the best sheep from his flock and gave it to God and God was very pleased with Abel.

Cain also worked hard to help Adam and Eve but he was not so worried about pleasing God. Cain did not give God what He asked for, and so God was not pleased with Cain[2].

As a result, Cain was angry and became jealous of his brother. Then, one day, when Cain and Abel were both out in the fields together Cain killed his brother Abel. God saw this. God punished Cain for his wicked act and said Cain would now find it even harder to dig the ground, to get rid of the weeds and grow his food. So Cain set out, and journeyed far away; away from everything he knew, to a new land, to start all over again.

After some years the area where Adam and Eve lived began to get crowded with their many children and grandchildren. The earth began to be filled with people. Some of them journeyed long distances so that they had enough room to live, to keep their flocks and grow their food.

Violence filled the earth

However, Satan had been watching all the things that Adam and Eve had done. He saw all the people that now lived on earth and he also saw Adam and Eve die, as God had said they would. He knew that one day he would also die, but this did not seem to worry him. He encouraged some of the other angels who lived in heaven to follow him and try to spoil what God had done.

These wicked angels then went down to earth and pretended they were men. They mixed with all the people on earth and some of them married the women of the earth. The children they produced grew up to be very big like giants. They were violent and wicked and this made everyone else violent. Soon all the people disobeyed God and did many wicked and evil things. God saw how bad everything was. He was very sad. He had made everything so good and He was grieved to see that Satan had spoiled many of the things which He had done.

God was so upset He began to wish He had not made man. God had wanted people to love Him and to be good to one another. Now He saw that men were becoming more and more wicked and that nearly everyone on the whole earth deserved to die. However, there was still one good man living on the earth. His name was Noah. He had a wife and three sons who were married. Noah loved God, and wanted to do good. God was very pleased with Noah and with his family.

The wicked angels had not influenced Noah and his family, and God saw that they did not deserve to die. He had a plan by which Noah and his family would be saved. God would make it rain for forty days and forty nights. He would make the oceans overflow and the waters become so high that they would cover all the land. Then all the wicked people would drown in these waters, and only Noah and his family would survive.

The flood

God told Noah to make a very large ship called an ark. He gave him many instructions as to how he should build it, and how big it was to be. God told Noah that He would send every kind of animal and bird into the ark when Noah had finished building it -so Noah knew why he had to make it so big.

After a long time, Noah finally finished building the ark, and when he had, God sent every kind of animal and bird into it, to save them all from drowning. Then Noah himself, with his wife and his three sons and their wives, went into the ark. As soon as everyone was safely inside and the doors were shut fast the rain began to pour down from the skies and the oceans overflowed. Soon, the ark began to float on top of the waters.

The rain poured down for forty days and forty nights. The ark floated on top of the waters and went wherever the winds blew it. At last the winds stopped blowing so hard. The rain stopped pouring down from the skies. Slowly the waters over the earth went down and after seven months the ark came to rest on the mountains of Ararat.

After ten months the tops of other mountains became visible, and after another forty days Noah opened the window he had made in the ark and sent out a raven. Until the water dried up, it just flew back and forth, finding no place to rest. Then Noah sent out a dove but it returned to the ark as the water was still over the surface of all the earth.

Seven days later Noah sent out the dove again, and this time it came back with a freshly plucked olive leaf in its beak. So after another seven days Noah sent the dove out again, and this time it did not return.

After one whole year of being in the ark, the water finally dried up from the earth. Noah removed the covering from the ark, but they had to wait another two months before the earth was dry enough for them to come out. So Noah, his family, and all the animals finally came out of the ark after spending one year and two months inside it. It came to rest on Mount Ararat and they were all very glad to be on dry land once again.

The rainbow

Noah opened the door and stepped out. No other people were left on earth except himself, his wife, his three sons and their wives. Noah let out all the animals and they were very glad to be on dry land once again.

Noah was very thankful that God had told him to build the ark to save his family and all the animals and birds. He built an altar to the Lord and made a sacrifice to Him which pleased the Lord. Then God blessed Noah and his sons and made a covenant with them.

A covenant is a special agreement between God and man. God promised that never again would He flood the *whole* earth and destroy *all* life. As a sign of this agreement He put a rainbow in the sky, and said that every time He saw the rainbow appear among the clouds this would remind Him of His covenant with all mankind.

We can still see the rainbow in the sky today when the sun shines into falling rain. This shows us how God has kept His promise and He will never again flood the whole earth with water. God always keeps His promises because He is good and righteous, and can always be trusted.

So Noah began his life all over again. He and his family were a little like Adam and Eve, who had to start all over again when God shut them out of the Garden of Eden, many years before.

****

Noah and the Flood

Questions

1. Why did God send a world-wide flood?
2. How do we know God will never send another world-wide flood?
3. What is a sacrifice?

Main references

Genesis 4:4   Abel offers a sheep to God

4:8   Cain kills Abel

4:12   Punishment of Cain

6:2   The wicked angels, called Sons of God,
appear on   the earth

6:4-5   Their children are born giants and are wicked

6:8-9   Noah is good

7:2-3   The animals go into the ark

9:11-17 The rainbow and God's promise

Please read now, or after you have read this book: Genesis 4-9

God's Plan so far

God
Heaven - and all the angels
Satan
Earth - and all animals
Adam and Eve
Cain and Abel
Noah and the flood

3. The Tower of Babel and God's New Plan
(Genesis 9-15)

Noah began his life all over again on the earth which had been destroyed by the flood. The only people alive on the earth were Noah and his wife, his three sons and their wives - just eight people.

However, as time went by and many years passed, the earth began to be filled with people again. All the people spoke the same language and everyone understood everyone else. People could easily discuss their ideas with all those around them and therefore they quickly came to know and understand many things.

The Tower of Babel

One day some of the people decided to use the ideas they had to build a tower. It was not an ordinary tower. They intended to build it with a top[3] like the sun, the moon and the stars. From this the people thought they could tell what would happen in the future - something God did not want them to do. God knew this would be bad for them and cause them a lot of trouble.

God looked down on this tower which the people were building, and He was not pleased with what He saw. After all, it was God who created the sun, the moon and the stars in the beginning. People used their time and energy to build this tower, hoping to make a name for themselves. Perhaps they wanted to be famous by trying to predict when there would be another flood.

However, God wanted them to get to know Him better, and to trust Him that He would never flood the earth again. He wanted them to discover all the good things He had done, and He wanted them to be kind to one another.

While God was looking down on the tower which the people were building, He decided to make all the people on earth speak different languages. Then the people would no longer be able to discuss their ideas with each other so easily. They would no longer be able to understand what everyone else was  saying. This meant they would have to spend years in learning other languages before they could discuss their ideas and work out the future, so the tower no longer had any use. It was called the Tower of Babel because it was there that the Lord confused the language of the whole world.

As a result of there being so many languages, groups of people who spoke the same language went to live in different places and became different nations. The population was scattered over the earth and since that time there has never been such a tower built again.

Many people found new lands where they settled down to live. Some of these people tried to please God by worshipping Him and these lived happy lives. However, some of the people did not want to worship God. They continued in their wicked ways for many years and Satan was pleased with them. He liked to lead people away from God whenever he could.

What God really wanted was for everyone on earth to learn about Him, to love Him, and to be good to each other. He wanted them to do as He wished so that everyone would then live happy lives and no one would be hurt. However, whenever God left the people on earth to do what they wanted to do there were always some who chose to go their own way and refused to obey God.

Abraham

It was then God began a new plan. He chose one man, called Abraham, and told him about His plan. Abraham was to be the father of a great nation of people who would one day go out to everyone else in the world and tell them all about God.

Abraham was married to a woman called Sarah, and together they followed God's instructions. First He told them to leave their own country and all the people they knew. They were to travel from Ur to a land which God would show them. They packed up all their belongings, and set out on a long journey from where they lived to the land of Canaan, which God led them to. Abraham was seventy-five years old when they moved to the land of Canaan, and yet he and Sarah still had no children. So Abraham wondered how he could be the father of a great nation of people as God had promised.

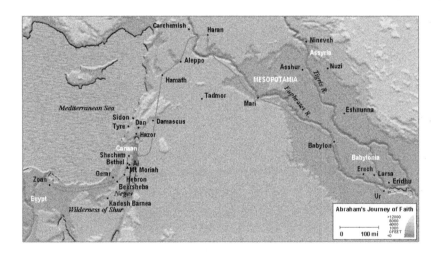

One night God spoke to Abraham. He told him to look up at the heavens and count the stars, if he could. Of course, there were too many for Abraham to count. God told Abraham that the same would be true of his descendants. Abraham believed God. He believed that he would be the father of a nation of people who would become so large that no-one would be able to count them.

God made a special agreement, called a covenant, with Abraham. He said He would give Abraham's descendants a large piece of land to live in - all the way from the river Nile in Egypt to the river Euphrates.

Abraham believed all that God had told him. He was happy to know that through him and his descendants, one day the whole world would learn about God and His great love for all the people He had made.

****

The Tower of Babel and God's New Plan

Questions

1. How were the different nations of this world formed?
2. God chose one man to be the beginning of a new plan for people on earth. What was his name?
3. What were the two main promises God made to this man?

Main references

Genesis 11:1   Everyone spoke the same language

11:4   The Tower of Babel is built

12:1   God chooses Abraham

12:2-3 Abraham to start a great nation

15:18 The land to stretch from the Nile to the Euphrates

Please read now, or after you have read this book: Genesis 9-15

God's Plan so far

God

Satan and the angels

Heaven and earth

Adam and Eve

Cain and Abel

Noah and the flood

The Tower of Babel

God's new plan

Abraham and the Promised Land

4. Abraham, Isaac and Jacob

(Genesis 16-37)

God first spoke to Abraham about His plan for him when he was seventy-five years old. Abraham wondered how this plan would come true, as he and his wife Sarah had no children. Later God spoke to him again about this plan. He told Abraham that his descendants would be as many as the stars in the sky, and that He would give them a large piece of land to live in - the country between the river Nile in Egypt and the river Euphrates.

The promised child - Isaac

When Abraham was ninety-nine years old, God spoke to him again and repeated His promise, His covenant, a third time. However, by this time Abraham and his wife Sarah were too old to have children, but then God worked a miracle.

When Abraham was one hundred years old, and Sarah was ninety, they had a son and they called him Isaac. They were both very pleased and very happy when Isaac was born. They loved Isaac very much and they knew that finally they had been given the child that God had promised them.

After some years God wanted to strengthen Abraham's faith by testing him. God asked Abraham to take his only son Isaac to the top of a mountain and offer Isaac as a sacrifice to God. This meant he had to kill his son. So Abraham, because he was a faithful man, decided to do what God had asked him to do although this was very hard.

Abraham knew that God had promised that he should be the father of a great nation of people. Abraham also knew that this would come about through Isaac's children and now God had asked him to sacrifice Isaac. But Abraham had such great faith in

what God had promised that he believed that if he killed Isaac, God would raise Isaac from the dead and bring him back to life again[4]. This is what he knew God must do if He was to keep His promise.

 So Abraham set out with Isaac to the top of the mountain. He laid Isaac down and took out a knife to kill him. But just as he was about to do this, an angel spoke to Abraham and told him not to kill Isaac after all. God was very pleased with Abraham because of his great faith and obedience. Abraham's faith had grown and Isaac's life was spared. Abraham killed a ram on top of the mountain as a sacrifice to God instead of his only son Isaac.

Isaac and Rebekah

When Isaac grew up he married a woman called Rebekah. For many years they had no children. Isaac however knew all about God's promise to bless his family and make them a great nation, so he asked God for a child. Soon Rebekah found she was expecting twins.

In those days the elder son inherited all the family rights and privileges. These included what was called the birthright and the special position of being the head of the family and God's priest for the family. However, before the twins were born, God told Rebekah that the younger one was to become the head of the family. He also told her that it would be through the younger that God's promises to Abraham would come true.

The twin boys were born - first Esau, and a few moments later Jacob, clutching on to Esau's heel! As they grew, Esau became a skilful hunter and loved to be outdoors, whereas Jacob was quiet and stayed near the tents where they lived. Isaac loved Esau best, but Rebekah loved Jacob.

Jacob and Esau

One of Jacob's greatest desires was to have the birthright and serve God. This birthright properly belonged to his brother Esau as he was the elder. Jacob knew that if he had the birthright, not only would he get a double portion of all their father's  possessions, but that he would also be entitled to get his father's blessing and be the head of the family and be God's priest for the family.

So one day when Esau arrived home very hungry and saw that Jacob was cooking some stew, Jacob seized his opportunity. When Esau asked for some stew, Jacob bargained with him, and told him he could have some stew as long as he promised to sell him his birthright. Esau hastily agreed as he was so hungry and he didn't really care at all about his birthright and serving God. Maybe Rebekah told Jacob what God had told her before the children had been born and so Jacob may have been anxious to hurry God's plan along.

Later, when Isaac was very old and could no longer see, he told Esau one day that he wished to give him his blessing before he died. Rebekah overheard her husband, and worked out a plan to make sure that Jacob received the blessing instead. She dressed

Jacob in Esau's clothes. Then she put skins on his arms to make him feel hairy like Esau. Finally, she sent him in to Isaac with a special stew which he loved to eat.

As Isaac was blind, he did not know it was Jacob with him instead of Esau, and so Jacob received his father's blessing. So God's message to Rebekah came true, and the younger son Jacob became the head of the family.

However, this was not the way that God had wanted it to happen. God is always sad when people are dishonest, or try to cheat one another.

The twelve sons

It was through Jacob that God's promises to Abraham were fulfilled. God changed Jacob's name to Israel. Later he had twelve sons who were the very beginning of the twelve tribes of Israel.

Therefore, at the beginning of God's plan to make a great nation of people to be a Kingdom of priests, who were to serve God, there were three very important men. These were Abraham, Isaac and Jacob. The twelve sons of Jacob all had children themselves and gradually more and more people were born and this nation of Israel became larger and larger. God had promised that Abraham would be the father of a great nation and slowly this was coming true.

****

The Twelve Sons

Jacob had his name changed to *Israel* and he had twelve sons. The sons became the fathers of the *Twelve Tribes of Israel*. The name of each son is given below, but the name has been scrambled into an anagram. See if you can unscramble it. If you need help, you can find all the names in Genesis 49.

run bee	me is on	vile	had ju
ben zulu	as his car	and	dag
rasher	a thin pal	hoe pjs	jab men in

Abraham, Isaac and Jacob

Questions

1. Why did Abraham take his only son Isaac to the top of a mountain to sacrifice him?
2. What did he sacrifice instead of Isaac, and why did he change his mind?
3. Why did Jacob want the birthright?
4. Why did Esau sell it to him?

Main References

Genesis 21:2   Birth of Jacob
        22:2   God asks Abraham to sacrifice Isaac
        22:13   Abraham sacrifices a ram instead
        25:24-26 Birth of Esau and Jacob
        27:28-29 Isaac gives Jacob his blessing

Please read now, or after you have read this book: *Genesis 21-27*

God's Plan so far

God
Satan and the angels
Adam and Eve;
Cain and Abel
Noah and the flood
The Tower of Babel
God's new plan
Abraham and the Promised Land
Isaac and Rebekah
Jacob (Israel) and Esau
Israel and his twelve sons

5. Joseph in the Land of Egypt
(Genesis 37-50)

Jacob had twelve sons, but one of these sons he loved more than all the others. His name was Joseph. He gave Joseph a beautiful cloak of many colours to wear, which Joseph was very pleased with. Joseph's older brothers did not like him being their father's favourite son, and they became very jealous of Joseph and hated him.

 One day, when Joseph was seventeen, he had a dream which he told his brothers about. He dreamed they were all binding sheaves of grain together. Suddenly his sheaf stood up straight, while all their sheaves gathered round and bowed down to his!

Another day Joseph had another dream which he also told his brothers. He dreamed the sun, the moon, and eleven stars were bowing down to him. When he told his father this dream, Jacob rebuked him and asked whether he really thought that one day his mother and father and brothers would actually bow down to him. Joseph had no way of knowing that this would in fact come true, and was all part of God's plan for both him, and all his family.

A short while later Jacob sent Joseph to his brothers who were away from home, out in the fields looking after the animals. They were looking after Jacob's flocks of sheep, and he wanted to check that all was well with them. When they saw him coming they planned to kill him, but Reuben, the eldest brother, persuaded them not to kill him. He suggested they threw him into a large hole in the ground instead. Just after they did this, they noticed some foreign men riding by, on their way to Egypt with spices to sell.

Joseph sold as a slave

So the brothers decided to sell Joseph as a slave to these men. They took the money, and poor Joseph became a slave and was taken to Egypt to work. Joseph's brothers dipped his cloak in goat's blood and took it to their father Jacob. When he saw it he thought that Joseph had been killed by a wild animal and was very sad.

When Joseph arrived in Egypt an officer of Pharaoh the King, called Potiphar, decided to buy him as a slave for himself. Potiphar was a very rich man and had everything he wanted. God was with Joseph in everything he did. When Potiphar realised this and saw how successful Joseph was in managing everything he was given to do, Potiphar put him in charge of his whole household. But Potiphar had a wicked wife. She lied about Joseph to her husband. Potiphar believed her and threw Joseph into prison.

However, God was still with Joseph even when he was in prison. The man in charge of the prison came to trust Joseph and put him in charge of all the other prisoners.

More dreams

Some time later Pharaoh, the king of Egypt, sent his chief cupbearer and his chief baker to prison for displeasing him. Joseph was put in charge of them too. One night they both had dreams, and in the morning Joseph asked why they looked so sad. It was because no-one could tell them what their dreams meant. Joseph told them God knew, and asked them to tell him their dreams.

The cupbearer dreamed that he squeezed the juice from bunches of grapes into Pharaoh's cup, and put the cup in Pharaoh's hand. Joseph told him this meant he would get his old job back. He also asked the cupbearer to mention him to Pharaoh when he was working for him again. In this way Joseph hoped to be freed from prison.

Joseph also told the baker what his dream meant. He had dreamed that birds were eating out of baskets of bread on his head. Joseph told him that this meant Pharaoh was going to kill him.

Everything happened just as Joseph had said, but the cupbearer forgot all about Joseph once he was free again, and did not mention him to Pharaoh as Joseph had hoped.

Pharaoh's dreams

Two years later the Pharaoh of Egypt had two dreams and he did not know what they meant. He was very troubled by his dreams, and asked many people whether they could interpret them for him. But no one could give him an answer.

Then, one day, the cupbearer remembered that there was a man called Joseph in prison who would be able to tell the Pharaoh what his dreams meant. So Joseph was taken to the palace, and stood before the Pharaoh of Egypt himself.

Pharaoh told Joseph about his two dreams. In his first dream there were seven very fat and lovely cows. Then seven very thin and ugly cows came along and ate up the seven fat cows. In his second dream there were seven good and healthy ears of corn. Then seven thin and scorched ears of corn grew up and swallowed the seven healthy ears of corn.

God had given Joseph the ability to interpret dreams, so he knew straight away what these dreams meant. He told Pharaoh that there would be seven very good years of harvests for the farmers. There would be lots of corn and plenty of everything for everyone to eat. This would be followed by seven years of famine. These seven years would be very bad, and everyone would be hungry because nothing would grow very well at all. Joseph also told Pharaoh what he needed to do to prepare for the seven years of famine.

Pharaoh was very pleased that Joseph knew what his dreams meant, and he rewarded him. He put him in charge of his palace and the whole land of Egypt. He made Joseph his second-in-command.

Joseph worked hard for the Pharaoh and the people of Egypt over the next seven years. Pharaoh allowed Joseph to do what he thought was best. Joseph built huge barns and told everyone in the land of Egypt to save a portion of their harvests for the next seven years. They were to store this away for the seven years of famine, when little food would grow. The people did as Joseph said and saved a lot of food and stored it all away.

At last the seven years of famine came. Everyone in the lands around Egypt became very hungry. However, the people in Egypt were not hungry as they had saved their food because Joseph had told them to.

Many people came to Egypt to try to buy food. Among these were Joseph's ten older brothers, who came from the land of Canaan. They were also very hungry and came to get some food to take back to Jacob their father.

When Joseph's brothers arrived in Egypt, they did not recognise Joseph. They had sold him when he was only seventeen years old, and now he was a man of forty-four. He was also the most important person in Egypt apart from Pharaoh himself.

The brothers bowed down low to Joseph with their faces to the ground and asked him to sell them some food. And so Joseph's dream of many years ago came true. His brothers bowed down to him, although they did not yet know it was Joseph.

Joseph however did recognise his brothers and gave them the grain they asked for. He also told them that if they returned to Egypt, they were to bring their youngest brother, Benjamin, with them.

Benjamin comes to Egypt

The next year, the second year of the famine, they had to return to get more food, and so they brought Benjamin with them. Once again, they bowed down before Joseph, without realising who he was. Joseph gave them the grain they asked for, but he also hid his silver cup in Benjamin's bag. When the brothers set off for home, Joseph sent his servant to overtake them, and search their bags. The cup was found, and Joseph commanded that Benjamin should stay and become his slave.

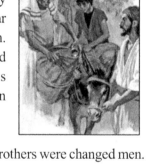

For the third time the brothers threw themselves to the ground in front of Joseph and pleaded that they should be his slaves as well. They could not bear to go home to their father without Benjamin. Jacob still thought that Joseph was dead, and Benjamin, the very youngest brother, was now his most beloved son. If Benjamin did not return home, they knew their father would die of grief.

Joseph could see that after these many years his brothers were changed men. They were no longer the jealous brothers they had once been, but wished to protect their youngest brother, and keep him safe, even if it meant they had to be slaves themselves.

Joseph forgave his brothers for all their past wickedness. He told them who he was, and at first they could not believe he was really Joseph. Joseph told them not to be afraid, as God had been with him all these years.

God had planned that he should go to Egypt so that he could help save many lives, including theirs, so that the people of Israel would survive. It was God who had sent Joseph his dreams of his brothers bowing down to him many years ago, and it was God who had made sure everything had happened to save the people of Israel from dying during the famine.

Jacob comes to Egypt

Joseph then asked them to go back and get their father, and bring him to live in Egypt. So his brothers went back to Canaan and brought Jacob to Egypt. Jacob was overjoyed to see

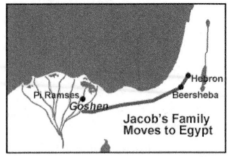

Joseph again after thinking for so many years he was dead. He was delighted to see that his favourite son was really alive, and that he had not been killed by a wild animal after all.

So all of Jacob's family, the people of Israel, came to live in Egypt. There they had plenty to eat, and were treated well by the Egyptians. They had many children, and these children had many children themselves, and so the nation of Israel, which started with Abraham, gradually got very large, and all of these people lived in Egypt.

****

Dreams: True or False

Is it *True* or *False* that Joseph or the cupbearer or the baker or the Pharaoh dreamt about these things? In other words, it is 'false' if none of them dreamt about such a thing.

Subject	True or False	Subject	True or False
sun		birds	
moon		bees	
meteors		cups	
stars		saucers	
comets		mugs	
grapes		horses	
bananas		cows	
coconuts		sheaves	
toast		barley	
bread		corn	

Joseph in the Land of Egypt

Questions

1. What two dreams did Joseph have when he was just seventeen years old?
2. How did they come true?
3. Why did the Pharaoh of Egypt ask to see Joseph?
4. Who sent Pharaoh his dreams?
5. How did Joseph discover his brothers were changed men?

Main References

Genesis	37: 1-11	Joseph's dreams
	37:12-36	Joseph sold as a slave
	39: 1-20	Potiphar and his wife
	40: 1-23	The cupbearer and the baker
	41: 1-40	Pharaoh's dreams
	41:41-57	Joseph becomes second-in-command in Egypt
	42: 1-38	Joseph's brothers go to Egypt
	45: 1-28	Joseph makes himself known
	46: 1-7	Jacob's family moves to Egypt

Please read now, or after you have read this book: Genesis 37-46.

God's Plan so far

God
Adam and Eve; Cain and Abel
Noah and the flood
Abraham, the Promised Land
Isaac; Jacob (Israel) and his 12 sons
Joseph and his dreams; Joseph in Egypt
Pharaoh and his dreams; the famine
Joseph's brothers go to Egypt
Jacob and all his family go to Egypt

6. Moses leads the People of Israel out of Egypt
(Exodus 1-15)

After many, many years a foreign king came and took over Egypt. This foreign king then became the new Pharaoh, but as he did not know of Joseph, and as he was a hard man, he was not pleased that there were so many people of Israel living in Egypt. He decided to make them all slaves to the Egyptians and to treat them very badly.

Later, this new Pharaoh decided that he did not want the number of the people of Israel to grow any larger. He ordered that all the Israelite baby boys should be thrown into the river Nile to drown just after they were born. However, God was still with the people of Israel, and just as He had led them safely into Egypt, He now had a plan which would lead them safely out of Egypt - to freedom once again!

One boy was saved from drowning. His mother put him in a little basket and floated him on the river in the hope that someone would find him and look after him safely. The daughter of the Pharaoh found the little baby and decided she would save him. She called the baby Moses. So Moses was saved from death, and brought up as an Egyptian. He lived in the palace, and grew up among the royal family.

Moses the man

When Moses grew up God chose him to lead His people. Moses loved God, but he was a quiet man who was meek and humble. So when God chose him to lead His people, at first Moses made many excuses as He thought that there must be someone better than himself to do God's work. But God knew that Moses was the right man to choose, and so Moses finally agreed.

One day God led Moses to the mountain of Horeb where he saw a brightly burning bush. From the middle of the burning bush came a loud voice. It spoke to Moses and told him that he would be the one to set all the people of Israel free from Egypt. This was God's voice. God told Moses to go to the Pharaoh of Egypt and ask him to let the people of Israel go. God knew that the Pharaoh of Egypt would not like the idea of letting the people go, because they were good slaves to the Egyptians. But God was on their side, and would help Moses to set free His people from suffering and slavery.

Ten plagues

So Moses went to the Pharaoh of Egypt and asked him to let the people of Israel go. When the Pharaoh would not agree to do so, God gave Moses the power to change all the water in Egypt to blood. So Moses changed all the rivers, lakes, streams and pools into blood. There was no fresh water to be found anywhere. Pharaoh was surprised at this, but although he was troubled by this miracle, he still did not let the people of Israel go free.

So Moses went to the Pharaoh again, and asked him to let his people go. Again Pharaoh hardened his heart and would not agree to do this. So this time God helped Moses bring a plague of frogs to the land of Egypt. There were so many frogs that the whole land of Egypt was covered with them and they were everywhere. It was a horrible plague. However, Pharaoh would still not agree to free the people of Israel.

Moses went to him again to ask for his permission to let his people go. This happened many times, and each time Pharaoh hardened his heart against the people of Israel. God helped Moses to bring another plague to the land of Egypt. The third plague was one of many lice, which came and crawled over every person and animal living in Egypt.

Then came the fourth plague. Millions of flies swarmed everywhere and made everything black. During the fifth plague the animals became sick and died. The sixth plague came and everyone in Egypt broke out in boils, so they could hardly stand. Then came  the seventh plague where thunder and hail were sent from the sky, and the hail was so heavy that the people and animals outside were killed. The eighth plague was locusts. There were so many locusts that they ate everything in Egypt. They ate every tree, and every bush and every flower, and every blade of grass, and all the crops. When they finally went away, there was no vegetation left at all. Then came the ninth plague of a thick darkness. It was so dark that no one could see anything at all for three days. Everyone stayed in their own homes. The sun did not appear, and it was like the blackest of black nights for three whole days.

These plagues were very terrible. But the Pharaoh was such a wicked and stubborn man that he deserved all these plagues. He would not believe in God or listen to him, and he would not let the people of Israel go. Even when all these plagues were over, Pharaoh still had a hard heart. He still would not let the people of Israel go out of Egypt to worship God
.

All these plagues proved that God was the true God of the earth as these plagues attacked the things which the Egyptians worshipped. The Egyptians worshipped their great river the Nile -but God turned it into blood. They also worshipped the sun, but God turned everything to darkness for three days. This showed that there was no other God but Him - the true God. He could control the sun and the rivers. There is only one God, and He is the only one to be worshipped.

The Egyptians also worshipped the Pharaoh and believed him and his first-born son to be gods. God did not want people to worship other people. Neither did He want them to worship the rivers or the sun, or animals, or anything else. He wanted everyone to worship Him. He is the only true God. He created all things and so He is the only one who should be worshipped. So after all these plagues God was sad that Pharaoh still would not let His chosen people, the people of Israel, go out of Egypt to worship Him.

The last plague

At last God came to the most terrible plague of all. He told Moses to tell all the people of Israel to kill a lamb - every family was to kill one lamb - and to put the blood on their doors outside. He told them all to do this on the same day. Then that night, all the families throughout the whole of Egypt were visited by God. The doors which had blood on them, He passed over. But in the houses where the doors had not been smeared with blood, He killed the firstborn son and the firstborn of all the animals. This meant that at the end of that terrible night, all the Egyptian firstborn boys and animals had been killed. However all the firstborn children of Israel had been saved, as God passed over their doors.

To the people of Israel this became known as the first *Passover*. Every year since that day the people of Israel have celebrated the day of *Passover* and have given thanks that their firstborn had not been killed. The lambs that the people of Israel had killed had taken the place of their firstborn sons.

Freedom!

After this terrible night, the Pharaoh, whose firstborn had also been killed, at last let Moses take the people of Israel out of Egypt. They left the land taking all their belongings with them. They had been in Egypt for hundreds of years, and now they were free and were no longer slaves. So Moses led them out of Egypt into the wilderness.

As soon as they were gone, however, Pharaoh again hardened his heart against the people of Israel and followed them to bring them back. The people of Israel had just reached the Red Sea, and God gave  Moses the power to part the waters of the Red Sea, so that all the people could pass through the sea on dry land. As soon as they were all over, the waters closed again, so that Pharaoh and all the Egyptian soldiers following them were drowned in the sea. The people of Israel were saved, and were at last free from the bondage of Egypt. They had reached the wilderness and were no longer slaves. They were very pleased, and so was Moses.

They were so joyful that they all sang a wonderful song, and praised God together, and God looked down upon them and was pleased with His people - the people of Israel.

****

One possible route for the Exodus is shown below.

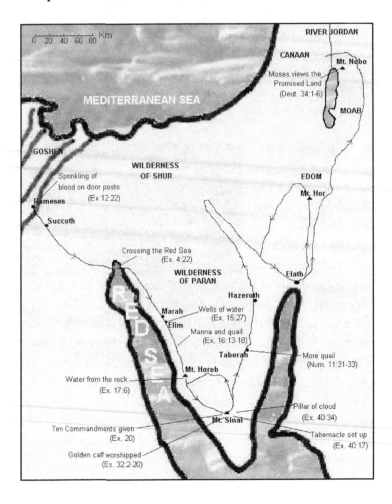

The Ten Plagues.

Can you remember them?

Exodus

7:20	1.	Water turned to _ _ _ _ _
8:6	2.	_ _ _ _ _
8:16	3.	_ _ _ _
8:24	4.	_ _ _ _ _
9:5	5.	All _ _ _ _ _ _ die
9:10	6.	_ _ _ _ _
9:23	7.	_ _ _ _
10:13	8.	_ _ _ _ _ _ _
10:22	9.	_ _ _ _ _ _ _ _
12:29	10.	All the _ _ _ _ _ _ _ _ males in Egypt die

Moses leads the People of Israel out of Egypt

Questions

1. Who brought Moses up?
2. Where was Moses brought up?
3. How did Moses persuade the Pharaoh of Egypt to let the
4. people of Israel go from Egypt?
5. What did the people of Israel celebrate on the day of Passover?

Main references

Exodus	1:8	A foreign king takes over Egypt (see also Acts 7:18)
	1:22 birth	All boys of the people of Israel to be killed at
	2:5-10	Moses is saved
	3:2	The burning bush

The Passover

Exodus	12:23	The Lord "passes over" the doors of the people of Israel
	12:41	The people of Israel left Egypt after 430 years
	13:3	The Passover - a day of celebration for the people of Israel (see also Luke 22:1)
	14:21	The Red Sea parted
	15:1-21	The people of Israel rejoice with a song

Please read now, or after you have read this book:

Exodus 1-3 and 7-15.

God's Plan so far

God
Adam and Eve
Cain and Abel
Noah and the flood
Abraham and the Promised Land
Isaac
Israel and his twelve sons
Joseph
Pharaoh and his dreams
Jacob and all his family go to Egypt
A new Pharaoh
Moses and the plagues of Egypt
The Passover and Crossing the Red Sea

7. From the Wilderness to the Promised Land

(Exodus, Leviticus, Numbers, Deuteronomy, Joshua)

The people of Israel were no longer slaves in Egypt. They wandered in the wilderness outside Egypt with Moses as their leader. God told Moses what to do, and Moses obeyed Him. God gave the people of Israel a sign to follow. By day there was a pillar of cloud in front of them which they followed, and by night there was a pillar of fire. Because they had this clear sign from God, they could never lose their way in the wilderness.

After a while the people became thirsty and they complained that they had no water. So God led them to a lake and to some wells in the desert where they could drink as much as they liked.

Then the people became hungry and complained that they had no food. They wished that they were back in Egypt as they had always had food to eat there. Although they were so ungrateful for their freedom, God decided to send them food, for they were His people and He would not let them starve. That evening He sent them birds, called quail, to eat and every morning He sent an unusual type of food called *manna*. It was very good to eat, and tasted delicious. So from that time onwards they were never hungry again.

The Law

Now in all we have heard so far, God has always spoken to certain people on the earth and told them what to do, and they have led the others. When Moses was in the wilderness with the people of Israel God gave them a set of rules to obey from that time onwards. They would then always know what they should do, and what they shouldn't do. Then God would no longer have to speak through a particular person, like Moses, and tell them what to do.

So God called Moses to meet and talk with Him on a mountain called Sinai. None of the other people of Israel were allowed to go up the mountain - so Moses went alone, and God spoke to him there. God gave Moses ten basic rules which are known as the *Ten Commandments*. They were very sensible rules, and Moses knew they were good because God had given them to him. God also gave him many other rules which all the people of Israel should follow. Moses remembered them all, so that he could tell the others when he came down from the mountain. These rules were known as *The Law*.

When God had finished giving Moses the Ten Commandments and all the other rules, Moses came down from the mountain. He told the people all the Lord had said to him and the people answered "Everything the Lord has said we will do." Then Moses wrote down all the rules the Lord had given him.

After that, God called Moses away again to tell him more about what He wanted His people to do. Moses left the people of Israel and once again went up the mountain to meet and talk with God. This time he was away for forty days and forty nights. God gave him many details of a special tent, known as a tabernacle, which Moses was to build. This tabernacle was to be a holy place. The word *holy* means something, or somebody, that is separated to God.

God gave Moses many more details about what the priests should wear, and what should be kept in the tabernacle, and on which days the people of Israel should perform certain ceremonies and worship God. God spent many, many days telling Moses what he and his people should do and how they should live. He also gave Moses two tablets of stone on which He had written the Ten Commandments, and when Moses returned to the people he took them with him.

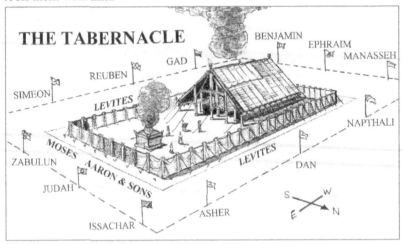

THE TABERNACLE

BENJAMIN
EPHRAIM
MANASSEH
GAD
REUBEN
SIMEON
LEVITES
NAPTHALI
MOSES
ZABULUN
AARON & SONS
LEVITES
DAN
JUDAH
ASHER
ISSACHAR

The Golden Calf

Meanwhile some of the people of Israel, without Moses there, began to turn away from God. They did not follow the new rules and regulations God had given them. Their behaviour grew worse and worse, so that when Moses came down from the mountain, he was very angry with what he saw. He threw the stone tablets to the ground and broke them into pieces.

These people had made a golden calf, and were worshipping it instead of God. All the people who were doing this were killed by the faithful ones, and a fresh start was then made. The people who were left once more tried to  keep the laws which God had given to them.

God told Moses to bring two new stone tablets and go up Mount Sinai to Him again. So Moses spent another forty days and forty nights on the mountain, and wrote down all that God said. When he returned this time, the people listened to all the Lord's commands, and saw the tablets on which He had written the Ten Commandments.

So God continued to lead His people through the wilderness, by the pillar of cloud by day, and the pillar of fire by night. And He led them in their lives by asking them to obey the Ten Commandments, and all the other rules He had given Moses on the mountain.

The Promised Land

Finally, the people of Israel reached the Promised Land. This was the land that God had promised many, many years ago to Abraham, Isaac and Jacob. He had promised that the people of Israel would have a land and a home of their own.

However, there were foreign tribes living in the land, and the people of Israel were afraid to enter it, because the men of these tribes were very big and also very good warriors.

Some men from Israel were chosen to go into the Promised Land to see what it was like. They came back with reports that it was an excellent land, flowing with milk and honey. Everything grew well there, and there was plenty to eat and drink. However, they also told the people about the large and fierce men living in the land.

So the people of Israel were afraid and did not believe God when He said He would be with them and help them to fight the fierce tribes there and win the battles. Only two of the men who had been sent to spy out the land had enough faith in God to believe that He would help them fight their battles. These two men were Caleb and Joshua.

God was angry with the people because they did not believe His words, and so He punished them. He said He would let them continue to wander in the wilderness, until all those who did not believe died. He would let only their children enter into the Promised Land with Joshua and Caleb, because all the others had disbelieved.

The wilderness again

So the people of Israel were turned by God back into the wilderness until all the disbelieving people had died. After forty years of wandering in the wilderness all their children had grown up. At last they arrived back to the borders of the Promised Land. It was here on a high mountain at the edge of the land that Moses died. He saw the land from this mountain, but he never actually entered it.

So Joshua and Caleb were the two men who led the people of Israel into the Promised Land. God was with the people, so they easily overcame the fierce tribes living there, and at last God's promise had been fulfilled. The people of Israel were now in the land called Palestine, the land which had been promised to them so long ago when Abraham was alive.

Although the people of Israel had often disbelieved God, and kept turning back to wicked ways, God remained faithful and kept His promise. He brought them to the land He had promised. God always keeps His promises to people, even if they do wrong, for God is faithful and true to His word.

****

The Ten Commandments

Can you remember them?
You can find the answers in Exodus 20.

---

1. You shall have no other _ _ _ _ before me.

2. You shall not make for yourself an _ _ _ _.

3. You shall not _ _ _ _ _ _ the name of the _ _ _ _

   your _ _ _.

4. Remember the _ _ _ _ _ _ _ day by keeping it holy.

5. _ _ _ _ _ your _ _ _ _ _ _ and _ _ _ _ _ _.

6. You shall not _ _ _ _ _ _.

7. You shall not commit _ _ _ _ _ _.

8. You shall not _ _ _ _ _.

9. You shall not give _ _ _ _ _ testimony.

10. You shall not _ _ _ _ _.

From the Wilderness to the Promised Land

Questions

1. How did the people of Israel know where to go when they were in the wilderness ...
   a. by day?
   b. by night?
2. How did they know what to do and how to behave?
3. Why did the people of Israel wander in the wilderness for forty years before they finally entered the Promised Land?
4. Who were the two men who led them into the Promised Land?
5. Why were they allowed to lead them in?
6. What are the names of the first six books of the Bible?

Main References

Exodus	13:21-22	The pillar of cloud and pillar of fire
	16:12-15	Manna and quails to eat
	20: 2-17	The Ten Commandments
	24: 3	Moses writes the Law down
	32:27-28	The wicked people killed
	34:28-29	The Ten Commandments written on stone tablets
Leviticus		Details of the Law
Numbers	13:26-28	Report on the Promised Land
	14: 6-10	Joshua and Caleb are faithful
	14:30-34	Forty years of wandering in the wilderness
Deuteronomy		More details of the law
	34: 4- 5	Moses dies on the edge of the Promised Land
Joshua		The people of Israel enter the Promised Land

Please read now, or after you have read this book:

Exodus 13-16, 20, 24, 32, 34, Leviticus 23, Numbers 13 & 14, Deuteronomy 34, Joshua 1-6.

God's Plan so far

God

Adam and Eve; Cain and Abel

Noah and the flood

Abraham, Isaac, Jacob; The twelve sons

Joseph into Egypt; Jacob and all his family go to Egypt

Moses and the plagues of Egypt

The Passover; Crossing the Red Sea

The wilderness

The Ten Commandments and the Law

The Promised Land

8. Judges, Kings and Prophets

(A brief synopsis of the rest of the Old Testament)

At last the people of Israel finally reached the Promised Land - the land which God had promised to Abraham, Isaac and Jacob. So the first part of God's plan had come true; there was a large nation in the Promised Land.

The next part was to teach all the people of Israel the truth about God - to bring them to love and serve God as a nation and to do what He asked. Then when they were all doing what God wanted them to do, they would be sent out as a nation of priests to all the other people on earth to tell them about God and His goodness, and His wonderful plans for the earth.

Judges

However, as had happened many times before, the people of Israel turned away from God and did not do what He asked and did not believe what He said. A few of the people did believe God, and these people remained faithful and did what God wanted them to do. From these faithful few some became what were called *Judges*. One of the most well-known judges was Samson, famous for his strength.

They ruled and guided the people of Israel. They were important because they tried to lead all the other people of Israel back to God and His Law. They wanted the people to be faithful to God, and to do what He said.

Some people listened to the Judges, but others did not. At that time many of the people of Israel did what was right in their own eyes, not obeying God's Law. Never did the whole nation of Israel come to believe God. It was always only a few here and a few there who believed and who tried to live by the Law. For God's plan to work, the whole nation had to believe in Him and do what He asked. However, God remained patient with them and was willing to wait.

Kings

Years passed, and a boy called Samuel was born. When he was still only a young boy God spoke to him, and from that time on Samuel became a spokesman for God. He spoke to all Israel,  and was accepted as a prophet. A prophet was a person who was chosen by God to tell everyone else about God, and what He was planning to do.

Sometimes prophets told the people what was going to happen in the future. Sometimes prophets explained what was happening right there and then. Sometimes prophets reminded people what God had done in the past. Like the judges before him, Samuel guided the people of Israel.

Samuel had two sons, but they did not follow the word of the Lord like he did. So when Samuel was old the people of Israel asked him to appoint a king to rule over them.

Up to this time the people of Israel had never had a king; God had always been their King and their Leader. All the nations living around the Promised Land had kings, and so the people of Israel wanted to be like them. God was not pleased with this idea, as He was their true King and Leader and no-one could be better than God Himself. But the people of Israel wanted a man as their king and leader on earth, so that they could be ruled over. They wanted someone they could see to lead them into battle against their enemies.

So, although God was not very pleased with this idea, He allowed them to have kings to rule over them because it was what they wanted. He also had to let them learn by their mistakes. God warned them that they would not like their kings when they got them, and that God was the only king who could be fair and just and good and loving all of the time.

God chose a man called Saul to rule the people of Israel, and be their first king. God told Samuel to anoint him with oil. Samuel did so, and Saul became king.

 However, it was not long before Saul failed to follow the Lord's commands. Samuel told Saul that God had chosen another leader who was a man after God's own heart. This man was called David. God sent Samuel to anoint David with oil instead, but it was many years before David finally became king instead of Saul. He had to wait until after Saul had died.

David was a great king and many times he did what was just and right. However, he also did several things which displeased God, and he broke some of God's most important commandments. Afterwards however, David was always very sorry for the wrong he had done, and repented to God from the bottom of his heart. So God forgave him, and let him continue as king of Israel.

David also wanted to build God a Temple, where the people of Israel could worship Him. But God did not allow David to do this because of some of the things he had done. Instead He told David that his son, Solomon, would build the Temple.

After David died, Solomon became a great king in his place. Solomon also believed and trusted God, and God was very pleased with him. In fact God was so pleased with Solomon when he was a young man that He allowed him to ask God for whatever he wished. So Solomon, rather than asking for lots of money and power, asked for wisdom - and as a result Solomon became the wisest ruler who ever lived on earth. Even so, Solomon still sometimes did things which God was not pleased with - but when Solomon was truly sorry for the wrong he had done, God forgave him.

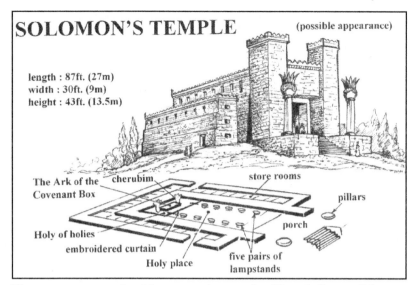

SOLOMON'S TEMPLE (possible appearance)

length : 87ft. (27m)
width : 30ft. (9m)
height : 43ft. (13.5m)

The Ark of the Covenant Box
cherubim
store rooms
pillars
porch
Holy of holies
embroidered curtain
Holy place
five pairs of lampstands

There were many other kings over the people of Israel. Some of these were good and tried to do what God wanted. Others were bad and did not bother about God and His Law. Even the good kings, as we have seen, still did some things which God was not pleased with.

This is because everyone who has been born since Adam is born with a character which always has some bad in it. This is called a *sinful nature*. We heard how Adam disobeyed God and ever since then, everyone has been born with a sinful nature, a character which is not completely good. However, some people decide to believe in God and trust in Him. They try to be obedient and follow Him. These people please God. Other people decide they will not believe in God nor follow His ways. These people allow the bad part of themselves to grow and as a result they do not please God.

Prophets

God looked down upon the earth, and saw that some of the kings were good and some of them were bad. He also saw that some of the people were good and some of them were bad. However, He saw that no one was perfect. He saw that no one was completely good all through.

What God wanted was for everyone to trust in Him and to try to be just like He is. If everyone had trusted in Him and followed His Law, then nothing would have gone wrong. In the first story, Adam would never have died if he had not sinned, and disobeyed God. Ever since then, everyone has been born with a sinful nature, and so everyone has died.

But God had a plan to save everyone from sin and death[5] - so that one day everyone who believes and trusts in Him, can be brought back to life, be perfect and live for ever. Then there will be no sin, and nothing will go wrong. There will be no more pain and suffering. There will be no more sin and death.

God's plan was to become a human Himself and to live on earth and die Himself. Under His Law the punishment for sin was death, so He would die in the place of all His people and bear the punishment for their sins. Doing this would enable Him to forgive all the sins they had ever committed. When God came He would be known as the Messiah, or the Christ. He also said that the Messiah would be born into the family of David.

Before God became a human Himself, He told some men on earth what He was going to do. These men were prophets, just like Samuel, and they lived about the same time as the kings we have just heard about. These prophets told the people of Israel about God's plan for the future, and they wrote these things down on scrolls. They told the people that God was going to become a man Himself, and that He would be born in Bethlehem, the City of David. They said that they would recognise God when He became a man because He would heal people of all their illnesses. And they told the people that He would save everyone who believed in Him from sin and death.

As usual, some of the people of Israel believed, and some of them did not. The people who believed were ready when God became a man on earth, and those who did not believe were not ready.

****

The Psalms

During this time all the Psalms were written. This is a collection of poems and songs. The most famous one is Psalm 23. How much of it do you know or can remember?

The LORD is my _____,

I shall not be in _____.

He makes me lie down in green _____,

he leads me beside quiet _____,

he restores my _____.

He guides me in paths of _____

for his name's sake.

Even though I walk through

the valley of the shadow of _____,

I will fear no _____, for you are with me;

your _____ and your _____,

they _____ me.

You prepare a _____ before me in the presence of my

enemies.

You anoint my head with oil;

my cup _____.

Surely _____ and _____ will follow me

all the days of my _____,

and I will dwell in the house of the LORD

_____.

Judges, Kings and Prophets

Questions

1. How did the Judges help the people of Israel?
2. Who chose Israel's first king of Israel?
3. Who anointed the first king?
4. What was the king's name?
5. What were the names of the next two kings of Israel?
6. What very special plan of God did the prophets tell the people of Israel about?

Main References

Judges	1-21	Details of the work of the Judges
	21:25	No king in Israel
1 Samuel	3:1-21	Samuel called by God
	8:6-7	God rejected as King
	10:1	Saul anointed king by Samuel
2 Samuel	5:3	David is anointed king
2 Samuel	12:24	Solomon is born
1 Kings	3:5-10	King Solomon asks God for wisdom
Isaiah	6:1-13	God warns that He will not bless Israel
	9:6-7	The birth of the Messiah foretold
	35:3-6	The healings of the Messiah foretold
	53:1-12	The suffering of the Messiah foretold
Micah	5:2	The Messiah to be born in Bethlehem

Please read now, or after you have read this book:

Judges 1-4, 1 Samuel 1-3 and 8-10; 2 Samuel 5 & 12; 1 Kings 3; Isaiah 6, 9, 35 and 53; and Micah 5.

God's Plan so far

God
Adam and Eve
Noah and the flood
Abraham, Isaac, Jacob
The twelve sons
Joseph into Egypt
Jacob and all his family go to Egypt
Moses and the plagues of Egypt
The Passover
Crossing the Red Sea
The Ten Commandments and the Law
The Promised Land
Judges
Samuel
Kings - Saul, David, Solomon
Prophets

9. The Lord Jesus is born
(Matthew 1 & 2; Luke 1 & 2)

God told the people of Israel that He would become a man Himself. He said He would come and live on the earth, so that He could die in their place and bear the punishment for their sins. In this way He could save them from sin and death, and could also save all those in the other nations of the world who believed in Him.

God said that when He became a man, He would be called Jesus, and would be known as the Messiah, or the Christ. However, as Jesus was both man and God, He is our Lord and so we call Him Lord Jesus. As we would expect, He never did anything wrong, He never said anything wrong, and He never thought anything wrong. He was perfect.

Mary and Joseph

His mother was called Mary, who was descended from King David. She was picked from all of the women in that family to be the mother of our Lord Jesus. God also chose a man called Joseph to look after Mary, and God told Joseph how he should help Mary.

God sent the angel Gabriel to tell Mary that she was to be the mother of the Messiah, and that she was to call Him Jesus. She replied that she was God's servant, and was happy for this to happen to her. An angel was also sent to Joseph to explain to him about the special baby that Mary was going to have. He was told not to be afraid to take Mary home as his wife, and to look after her carefully, as she was to be the mother of the Messiah. Joseph too was told that His name was to be Jesus, as this name meant that He was going to save His people from their sins.

Although the Lord Jesus is God, He was born in a very poor and lowly place. When He was born He was laid in a manger, in a stable in Bethlehem, a little village in Palestine. This shows that although God is such a great and wonderful God, He is also very humble. If Joseph and

Mary owned a donkey, it would have taken them about ten days to travel from Nazareth, where they were living, to Bethlehem, where Jesus was to be born.

The prophets had told the people of Israel that God would come down to earth. They had also told all the people what to look for, so they would know who the Lord Jesus was when He was born. The prophets had written all these things in books so everyone could know - but unfortunately only a few believed, and so only a few knew what signs to look for.

The shepherds and the wise men

There were some shepherds who belonged to the people of Israel. They looked after sheep in the fields. On the night after the Lord Jesus was born, some angels from God came to them in the fields. The angels told the shepherds that the Lord Jesus had been born, and that they should go and look for Him. These shepherds were some of the few that believed. They went to Bethlehem and found the Lord Jesus lying in a manger in a lowly stable. After they had seen Him, they went off and told many people what had happened. The people were amazed at what the shepherds said, and the shepherds returned to their fields glorifying and praising God.

Some time later, some wise men from a land a long way from Palestine, came to see the Lord Jesus. These wise men had seen a special star in the sky which told them that the Lord Jesus, the true King of the people of

Israel, had been born. They had journeyed a long, long way to come and see Him and they brought three gifts. One was gold, one was frankincense, and the other was myrrh.

Gold was a gift for a King, and Jesus was to be the King of the Jews. Frankincense symbolised purity, and Jesus was pure from sin from His birth to His death. Myrrh was a symbol of death, and Jesus was to die to save people from sin and death.

However, many of the people of Israel did not know He had been born, and some who did know did not believe that He was God[6]. They had no excuse, however, for not knowing and not believing. They had the books of all the prophets telling them about God and His plan.

One who did not believe was the king of Israel. His name was Herod. When he heard from the wise men that a child had been born who was to be ruler over Israel, Herod was afraid. He did not rejoice at the news, but instead planned to kill the child Jesus. He asked the wise men to return to him and tell him where to find the child so that he could worship Him. However, he really wanted to know where the Baby was so that he could kill Him.

The wise men were warned by God in a dream to return home without seeing Herod, so they did. Herod was furious, and in his rage he ordered that every boy of two years old and under who lived in and around Bethlehem was to be killed. But God had already sent an angel to Joseph to warn him of what was going to happen, so Joseph, Mary and the young Jesus left for Egypt immediately, and so Jesus was saved from death.

Some time later, after Herod had died, the family moved back from Egypt to Palestine and the Lord Jesus grew up in a town called Nazareth. He learned to be a carpenter like Joseph.

The temple in Jerusalem

When the Lord Jesus was twelve years old, He went with Mary and Joseph to Jerusalem. Every year many of the people of Israel went to Jerusalem to celebrate the Passover. This was the time of year when all the people remembered how - long ago - God *passed over* all their houses, and did not kill their firstborn sons, because a lamb had been killed instead.

So the Lord Jesus went to the temple in Jerusalem to celebrate the Passover. Although He was only twelve, He knew that He had been born to die in the place of many, many people, to save them from sin and death. Just as the Passover lambs had died in the place of all the firstborn sons so many years ago, the Lord Jesus knew that He was to die for the sins of the world. This great act of love was to save people from sin and death. It would allow God to give everlasting life and righteousness to all who believed and trusted in Him.

When Mary and Joseph and all their family and friends began their journey home to Nazareth from Jerusalem the Lord Jesus remained behind and began to talk to the old and wise men at the temple. They were amazed at His knowledge, as they thought that He was  only an ordinary child. They did not realise that He was also God.

When Mary and Joseph realised Jesus was not with them, they returned to Jerusalem and spent three days searching for Him until they found Him in the temple. He asked them why they hadn't known He would be in His Father's house, meaning the temple of God, but they didn't understand what He said. Then He went back with them to Nazareth. There He lived with them for many years in perfect obedience as a perfect Son.

When He was thirty years old, He knew it was time for Him to start teaching the people of Israel what God wanted them to know and do. Many times before, God had used men to tell Israel what He wanted them to do. Later God had made laws, including the Ten Commandments, to tell them what He wanted them to do. Now God had become a man and so at last He could tell them Himself what He wanted them to believe and do.

****

Possible route Mary and Joseph took from Nazareth to Bethlehem

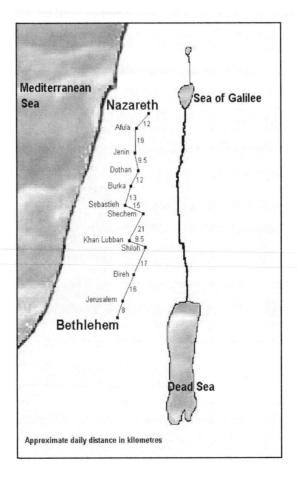

The Lord Jesus is born

Questions

1. How did the shepherds know where to find the baby Jesus?
2. How did the wise men know where to find the child Jesus?
3. Why didn't the wise men tell Herod where to find Jesus?
4. What three gifts did the wise men bring?
5. What did each gift signify?
6. Why were the old and learned men in the temple amazed at Jesus when He was only twelve years old?

Main references

Luke	1:26-39	Mary and Gabriel
Matthew	1:18-25	Joseph and Gabriel
Luke	2:1-5	Bethlehem
	2:6-7	Birth of the Lord Jesus
	2:8-20	Shepherds
Matthew	2:1-12	The wise men
	2:13-18	Off to Egypt
	2:19-23	Back to Nazareth
Luke	2:41-52	In the Temple

Please read now, or after you have read this book:

Matthew 1 & 2 and Luke 1 & 2.

God's Plan so far

Mary and Joseph
The angel Gabriel
Bethlehem
The Lord Jesus is born
The Shepherds
The Wise Men
Off to Egypt
Back to Nazareth
In the Temple in Jerusalem

10. The Miracles of the Lord Jesus

(Luke 3-7; John 2)

When the Lord Jesus was thirty He began speaking to the people of Israel. God had made an agreement with the people of Israel, and so the Lord Jesus was going to put His plan into action. Initially. This plan initially involved only the people of Israel, but when they were ready, they would then go to all the other nations on the earth. However, while the Lord Jesus was on earth He did not go to any of these other nations.

Before He began speaking to the people of Israel, the Lord Jesus was baptised by a man called John the Baptist in the river Jordan. When He came out of the river Jordan the heavens opened and the Holy Spirit came down on Him in the form of a dove. A voice from heaven said, "You are my son whom I love. I am well pleased with you." This was a sign to all the people of Israel that the Lord Jesus was truly God Himself. He was the One the prophets had spoken about.

The temptations

As soon as He had been baptised the Lord Jesus was led into the desert by the Holy Spirit. While He was there, the wicked angel Satan tried to tempt the Lord Jesus. First he told Him to turn a stone into bread to prove He was the Son of God. Jesus answered, "It is written, 'Man does not live on bread alone.'"

Then Satan told Him that if He would worship him, he would let Jesus have authority over all the kingdoms of the world. But Jesus answered, "It is written, 'Worship the Lord your God and serve him only.'"

For a third time Satan tempted Jesus. He told Him to throw Himself down from the highest point of the temple to prove that the angels would come and save Him. Jesus answered a third time, "It is written, 'Do not put the Lord your God to the test.'"

God had created Satan Himself at the very beginning, so of course the Lord Jesus did not need to prove Himself to Satan, nor would He ever worship someone He had made. The Lord Jesus told Satan to depart from Him, and so Satan had to give up. Each time Satan tempted Him, the Lord Jesus replied with a quotation from the written Scriptures. This shows that if people live by what the Scriptures teach, Satan's temptations will always fail. The first step, however, is to *know* what the Scriptures teach.

After this temptation in the wilderness the Lord Jesus began to do and say many wonderful things in the land of Palestine. He gathered around Him twelve men who believed what He said and who had faith in Him. One of these men was called Simon Peter, and he was a fisherman. These twelve men were known as the twelve disciples of the Lord Jesus, and they were all from the people of Israel.

The first miracle that Jesus performed was turning water into wine. He was invited to a wedding feast one day, and the people there had run out of wine. Jesus' mother mentioned this to Him, and so He turned six jars of water into wine of the finest quality. In this way He revealed His glory, and His disciples put their faith in Him.

Healing miracles

After this He performed many wonderful signs and miracles. He healed many people just by touching them. He felt sorry for them when He saw that so many were sick and dying. However, His main desire was for the people to believe in Him, and to believe that He could forgive them their sins and give them eternal life.

Healing people of their sicknesses was a sign that He could forgive them their sins. This was much more important than healing their bodies, as it meant that God could finally have what He had always wanted from the beginning. He wanted everyone to be perfect, just like He is - so if everyone's sins were forgiven and gone, and everyone would live forever, God would have a perfect creation.

One of the first people that Jesus healed was Simon Peter's mother-in-law. She had a bad fever, so he asked Jesus to help her. He came to her side, bent over her, told the fever to go, and it left her that moment. She got up straight away and started to wait on Jesus and His disciples.

Creation miracles

Not only did Jesus perform many miracles of healing, but He also showed He was Lord of the whole creation in many different ways. The first miracle He ever did showed this. That was when He turned water into wine.

Another day, many people were crowding around Jesus, wanting to listen to what He had to say. Jesus noticed two fishing boats nearby, and got into one with Simon Peter, asking him to push it out a little way from the shore. Then He taught the people from the safety of the boat.

When He had finished He told Simon Peter to let down his nets to catch some fish. Simon Peter told Him they had been fishing all night and caught nothing. Even so, as Jesus had asked him to, he let down the nets, and when he had done so they caught such a huge number of fish that the nets began to break. He called for the other boat to come and help them, and eventually both boats were so full of fish they began to sink!

 Peter was overcome at seeing this miracle. He realised just how great the power of the Lord Jesus was. He told the Lord Jesus to go away from him. Compared with Jesus, Peter felt so sinful that he was ashamed of himself. At that moment, Peter realised just how perfect and sinless the Lord Jesus was.

This is just what the Lord Jesus wants everyone to realise, as then they will see that they need Him to forgive them their sins.

More healing miracles

Not long after this the Lord Jesus healed a man who had a very serious illness called leprosy. This man believed in Him. He knew that not only could Jesus heal him from his leprosy, but also that He could forgive him his sins. When the Lord Jesus had done so He told the leper not to tell anyone else that He had healed him from his leprosy. Instead he should go straight to the priest and offer sacrifices. These were necessary because of the Law God gave to Moses, so that the leper could be pronounced clean by the priests, who would see that he had been completely healed.

Soon afterwards the Lord Jesus was talking to a crowd of people in a house. Four men arrived outside the house carrying a paralysed man on a stretcher. They wanted Jesus to heal the man. However, there were so many people in the house that they could not get through the door. So the four men carried the paralysed man up to the roof of the house, and lowered him down into the house through the roof.

When the Lord Jesus saw the paralysed man on the stretcher, and that there were many people all around watching Him, He told the man that his sins had been forgiven. But some of the people watching did not believe this at all, and wondered how the Lord Jesus could say such a thing. They all thought to themselves that it was easy enough to say to a person "your sins have been forgiven". But they also knew that it is only God who can forgive sins!

The Lord Jesus knew what they were thinking, and so He told them that He would heal the man from his paralysis as well. This was to show them that He was God, and therefore had the power both to heal and to forgive sins. When they saw that the paralysed man was completely healed and that he got up immediately, and walked home easily, they were amazed and began to believe and glorify God.

Saving miracles

Another day, the Lord Jesus met a tax collector called Levi, whose other name was Matthew. He told Levi to follow Him, so Levi did. Then Levi held a great feast at his house for Jesus and His disciples. He invited many other tax collectors and friends of his.

However, the Pharisees and teachers of the Law asked why Jesus and His disciples ate and drank with such sinful people. The Lord Jesus replied that He had come to earth so that He could save sinners like these. He had not come to spend His time with people who were perfect and did not sin! Jesus knew the Pharisees, and others like them, *thought* themselves perfect and righteous. However, no-one is perfect and righteous, except God Himself. So He sent the Lord Jesus to save those people who realise that they have sinned, and confess it to Him. All they have to do is to admit they are sinners and to believe that Jesus can save them.

Another time, a woman who many people knew had lived a very sinful life came to see the Lord Jesus. She realised she was a sinner, and wept over the feet of the Lord Jesus, and washed His feet with her tears. She dried them with her hair, and then poured oil all over His feet, as she realised how great He was. He saw that she believed in Him and He forgave her all her sins.

Raising the dead

One of the most wonderful miracles Jesus did early in His ministry was to raise a widow's son to life. One day Jesus went to a town called Nain, and arrived just as a dead person was being carried out in a coffin. His mother was following along crying: she was a widow. Jesus' heart went out to her and told her not to cry. Then He touched the coffin and told the young man inside to get up. He got up, and began to talk, and Jesus gave him back to his mother.

Everyone who saw this was filled with awe and praised God, and told everyone else that God had come to help His people. How right they were! As a result, the news about Jesus spread quickly throughout the surrounding villages and towns.

All of the people we have heard about up to this time were Israelites. God sent the Lord Jesus only to the people of Israel. He was to prepare them for their work of taking God's good news to all the other nations on earth. However, despite all His wonderful miracles only some of the people of Israel believed in the Lord Jesus.

****

Some of the places Jesus visited

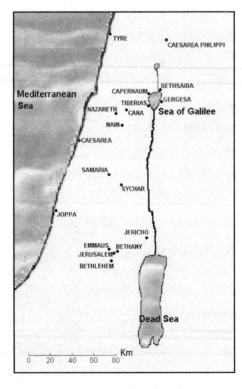

Introducing God's Plan   72

The Twelve Disciples

Can you name the Twelve Disciples?

To help you, see if you can unscramble them.
Their names are given in Luke 6:14-16.

1. e pert
2. wet math
3. new rad
4. maths O
5. same j
6. same j (son of) Saul Heap
7. no j h
8. I'm son to Zale
9. I phlip
10. ad jus (son of) am jes
11. the low rob ma
12. sad ju is to cari

The Miracles of the Lord Jesus

Questions

1. Did Jesus do what Satan asked Him to do?
2. If not, why not?
3. Which did Jesus think was more important - healing people from sickness, or giving them eternal life?
4. Why did Jesus heal people?
5. Which, do you think, was one of the most wonderful miracles Jesus did?
6. Why do you think it is the most wonderful?

Main references

Luke	3:21-22	Baptism of the Lord Jesus
	4:1-13	Temptation of the Lord Jesus
John	2:1-11	Turning water into wine
Luke	4:38-39	Peter's mother-in-law is healed
	5:4-6	Miracle of the fishes
	5:12-13	The leper is healed
	5:18-26	The paralysed man is healed
	5:27-32	The Lord Jesus visits a tax collector
	6:14-16	The names of the twelve disciples
	7:11	The widow of Nain's son is raised
	7:44-50	A sinful woman is saved

Please read now, or after you have read this book:

Luke 3-7 and John 2

God's Plan so far

Gabriel, Mary and Joseph
Jesus is born in Bethlehem
Shepherds and Wise Men
Off to Egypt
Back to Nazareth
John the Baptist
The Holy Spirit and the dove
Satan and the temptations
Peter and the twelve disciples
Healing miracles
Creation miracles
Raising the dead
Forgiving sins
Eternal life

11. The Lord Jesus is rejected

(Matthew 14,15; Luke 7,8,9; John 6,7)

All of the people we have heard about since the time of Abraham have been Jews, which is another name for the people of Israel. They are most important because they were, and still are, God's chosen people. Anyone who is not a Jew is called a Gentile - so all the other nations of the world are Gentiles. God's plan was that, one day, the Jews would go and tell the Gentiles all about God and how wonderful He is, and how He can forgive them their sins and give them eternal life. But, unfortunately the Jews were never faithful enough to God to begin to do this work.

In the last chapter we saw how some of the Jews believed in the Lord Jesus and were saved from their sins - but some of them did not believe in Him at all, especially the Pharisees and Sadducees. Although Jesus spent most of His time on earth with the Jews, He did occasionally come into contact with Gentiles, as a few Gentiles lived in Israel. Sometimes it seemed that these Gentiles had more faith than many of the Jews!

Gentiles

One day a Gentile who was a centurion, a Roman soldier, sent some Jewish elders to see the Lord Jesus. His servant was sick and almost dead, and he wanted the Lord Jesus to heal him.

When the Lord Jesus came near to his house, the centurion sent friends of his to meet Jesus, to ask Him not to go in. He said that he was not worthy to have the Lord Jesus in his house, or even to meet Him face to face. Although he was a Gentile, he knew just how great the Lord Jesus was, and he had great faith in Him.

The Lord Jesus knew this and said to all the people around that He had not found in all of Israel a man with such great faith. This Gentile man put the Jews to shame. Then the friends who had been sent by the centurion went back into the house, and found the centurion's servant was well.

Another day a woman who came from Canaan, who was also a Gentile, came to the Lord Jesus and asked Him to heal her daughter. The Lord Jesus told her that He had been sent to the people of Israel. (He was more concerned about helping them - so that they would then be ready to go out to the rest of the world.)

The woman was not offended by this. She knew that the Jews had a special place in God's plan, and that they must come first. However, she also knew God wanted the Gentiles to learn about Him through listening to the Jewish teachings. She knew that although the Jews had first place and had special blessings, yet the Gentiles had a place in God's plan and that He would bless them also. She told Jesus this and He marvelled at her faith.

She believed all that the Lord Jesus said, and He knew this. He told her how great her faith was, and then He healed her daughter. Compared with these Gentiles, the Jews' lack of faith and their unbelief appeared worse. They should have been ashamed of themselves.

Parables

Although the Lord Jesus tried for many days, and weeks, and months to help the people of Israel, and to teach them, many would not listen and believe. There was little point in telling them any more. The Lord Jesus decided that from then on, only those who wanted to listen and understand would be able to. Instead of saying exactly what He meant, He began to teach in parables.

A parable is a story which gets over a point by using examples. However, sometimes the examples used made what was said more difficult to understand, rather than easier. Sometimes the meaning had to be explained afterwards. The Lord Jesus told many parables, but only explained them to His disciples so that they would understand what He was saying. Many other people who heard a parable[7] thought it was a lovely story, but were not interested enough to ask the Lord Jesus what it meant.

When Jesus first started to teach, many people turned to Him and believed when they saw His miracles. However, now those miracles no longer seemed to have the same effect. Even His chosen twelve disciples wavered in their faith on some occasions.

 Sometimes His power made them puzzled and afraid. One day Jesus got into a boat with them to go across the lake. Soon He fell asleep. While He was sleeping a storm blew up, and the waves grew so rough they threatened to swamp the boat, and drown them all. The disciples were terrified, and frantically awoke Jesus. He immediately commanded the storm to stop, and the water became perfectly calm and still. The disciples still did not seem to realise just how powerful Jesus was, even though they had seen Him turn water into wine, help them catch an enormous number of fish, heal hundreds of people, and, most wonderful of all, raise a person from the dead. Instead they were fearful and amazed, and asked each other who Jesus could possibly be, if even the winds and the waves obeyed Him.

 Soon after this a man called Jairus, a ruler in a Jewish meeting house called a synagogue, came and pleaded for Jesus to come and see his daughter as she was dying. Before Jesus arrived someone from Jairus' house came to Him and announced that the girl was dead. Jesus told Jairus not to be afraid, and they went into his house, together with Peter, James and John - three of the twelve disciples. Jesus took the girl by the hand and told her to get up. The life returned to her and she immediately stood up. Both her parents were astonished. They could not believe that Jesus had the power to raise a dead person to life, and yet here they had seen it with their own eyes. However, this time Jesus told them not to tell anyone

what He had done. By now it was sad but true that few people put their faith and trust in Him as a result of seeing or hearing about His miracles.

Turning away

Another day the Lord Jesus miraculously provided food for a crowd of five thousand people to eat. They had been listening to His teachings for a long time and were hungry. A little boy had with him five loaves and two small fish. So Jesus took these, broke them in pieces and passed them to the disciples for them to hand out to everyone. He created enough food to feed the whole crowd, with twelve basketfuls left over besides.

Later that night His disciples were out on the lake in a boat when they saw Jesus walking towards them on the water. They were terrified, as they thought it must be a ghost. He called to them and told them not to be afraid, and so they took Him into the boat with them. Then they worshipped Him and knew that He was truly the Son of God.

However, next morning when many of the crowd who had been fed the day before returned to see Jesus again, He saw that they were not interested in His miracles and why He did them. All they wanted was to be fed again. When Jesus explained that He wanted to give them spiritual food which would last forever, many did not understand what He was saying. They could have everlasting life if only they would believe in Him and accept Him as their Saviour.

Instead, many of them turned away from Him and refused to accept His teaching. They were no longer His followers. Even His own brothers refused to believe in Him.

The transfiguration

However, although they often wavered in their faith, Jesus' twelve disciples remained with Him and tried to believe and understand all that He told them. One day three of the twelve - Peter, James and John - were with Jesus on a mountain. Suddenly, Jesus' face shone like the sun and His clothes became as white as the light.

Then they saw two other people standing with Jesus - Moses and Elijah - and they were talking together. Then a bright cloud surrounded all of them, and a voice spoke, the voice of God the Father, telling them that Jesus was indeed His Son and that they should  listen to Him. This was the same voice that came from heaven when Jesus was baptised, when the dove had descended from heaven.

The three men were terrified and fell on their faces to the ground. But Jesus touched them and told them to get up, and not to be afraid. Then things returned to normal, and Peter, James, John and Jesus went back down the mountain. Jesus told them not to tell anyone what they had seen until He had been raised from the dead.

However, they did not understand what He meant about being raised from the dead. They refused to believe that He was going to die. Jesus explained to them that it was necessary for Him to die, and that later He would rise from the dead. They could not seem to understand it, yet they should have understood.

Finally, when most of the people of Israel had rejected Him, and did not believe Him to be their Messiah and Saviour, it was time for Jesus to fulfil what He came to earth to do. He had come to die for the sin of the world; to die in the place of all sinners who believed in Him, to save them from sin and death.

So the day got nearer. He knew that His death was to take place near Jerusalem, so He began to make His way towards that city.

****

Parables

There are seven parables in Matthew 13.
Can you name them?

The Parable of the _ _ _ _ _

The Parable of the _ _ _ _ _

The Parable of the _ _ _ _ _ _ _   _ _ _ _

The Parable of the _ _ _ _ _

The Parable of the _ _ _ _ _ _   _ _ _ _ _ _ _ _

The Parable of the _ _ _ _ _

The Parable of the _ _ _

The Lord Jesus is rejected

Questions

1. How did the Gentile Roman centurion put the Jews to shame?
2. What is a parable?
3. Did the parables make Jesus' teaching easier or more difficult to understand?
4. How did the disciples understand the parables?
5. What was the main reason for Jesus coming to earth?

Main references

Luke	7:2-10	The centurion's daughter is healed
Matthew	15:22-28	The daughter of the Gentile woman is healed
Luke	8:9-10	Speaking in parables
	8:22-25	Calming the storm
	8:41-56	Jairus' daughter is raised from the dead
	9:12-17	Feeding of the five thousand
Matthew	14:22-32	Walking on the water
John	6:60-66	Jesus' followers turn from Him
	7:1-5	Jesus' own brothers do not believe in Him
Luke	9:28-36	The Transfiguration

Please read now, or after you have read this book:

Matthew 14 & 15; Luke 7, 8 & 9; and John 6 & 7.

God's Plan so far

Gabriel, Mary and Joseph
Jesus is born in Bethlehem
Shepherds and Wise Men
John the Baptist
The dove from heaven
Satan and the temptations
Peter and the Twelve
Miracles
Forgiving sins and eternal life
The Jews turn away
Parables
The Transfiguration

12. The Lord Jesus goes back to Heaven
(Luke 22-24; Acts 1)

When the Lord Jesus began to make His way towards the city of Jerusalem it was nearly the time of year for the Passover. It was the last time that He would take the Passover feast, as He knew the time for His death was drawing near.

His twelve disciples were with Him as He came near to Jerusalem. One of these was called Judas Iscariot. Although he had followed the Lord Jesus with the other eleven, he allowed Satan to influence him to tell the leaders of the people of Israel where the Lord Jesus was. These leaders did not believe in the Lord Jesus. They were afraid and jealous of His great power and authority. They wanted to capture Him and put Him to death, so they plotted to send their soldiers to arrest Jesus.

The Passover

The twelve disciples and the Lord Jesus found a room upstairs in a house where they could celebrate the Passover. While they were eating, the Lord Jesus told them that soon He must suffer and die. He said that one of the disciples sitting around the table with Him would betray Him to the leaders who did not believe in Him. He already knew that Judas Iscariot had planned to do this.

When the disciples wondered among themselves who this could possibly be, Judas pretended that he didn't know either. They also wondered who was the greatest among them, but the Lord Jesus told them that it wasn't important.

 Peter said he would always be faithful to the Lord, but the Lord replied that Peter would soon deny Him three times by pretending that he did not know Him. He also said that after this Peter would hear a cock crow. But Peter did not believe Jesus. He said he would never deny the Lord Jesus or say that he did not know Him!

After they had finished the Passover supper, the Lord Jesus went outside with His disciples. Meanwhile Judas Iscariot slipped off to tell the soldiers where they could find Him.

The Lord Jesus went to the Garden of Gethsemane at the foot of the Mount of Olives and began to pray. He asked the others to stay awake and pray with Him, but they were too tired and fell asleep. So He stayed awake alone, while He prayed. He knew that His death was not far away.

While He was praying, Judas Iscariot arrived with the soldiers and kissed the Lord Jesus. The kiss was a sign to the soldiers that this was the person they wanted. So they captured Jesus and led Him away to the house of the high priest who was the most important leader in Israel. There they questioned Jesus.

Most of the disciples were afraid, but Peter and John were brave enough to follow the Lord Jesus. When they reached the high priest's house they sat around a fire, and Peter sat among some other people while the Lord Jesus was being questioned.

Three times people asked him whether he knew the Lord, and whether he had been with Him. His answer each time was "No!" - he was afraid to admit that he was one of His followers. As soon as he had said "No!" the third time the cock crowed. The Lord Jesus turned to look at Peter - and Peter remembered what He had said. He was bitterly ashamed of himself and went outside and wept.

The Trials

When the high priest and the other leaders questioned the Lord Jesus, He told them He was God, and that He was the King of the Jews. They did not believe Him and called this blasphemy. Blasphemy is saying something bad or wrong about or against God. As the Lord Jesus is God He could never blaspheme. But because they did not believe He was God they wanted Him punished. They wanted Him to die, as they were afraid of His great power. They were afraid of whom He claimed to be and that the people might follow Him, rather than them.

So they took Him to the Roman ruler called Pilate who had authority to say who was guilty and who was innocent. He also had the power to put people to death - or to set them free. When the high priest and leaders told him about the Lord Jesus he told them he thought He was innocent and would let Him go. But they shouted at him and got crowds of people to cry for the death of the Lord Jesus.

The Crucifixion

So Pilate reluctantly said he would put the Lord Jesus to death. He only agreed to do this to avoid a riot.

The Lord Jesus was led away to a place called Calvary. A large wooden cross was placed in the ground and the Lord Jesus was nailed to this cross to die.

So the Lord Jesus accomplished what He came to earth to do. He died not as a result of His own sins, but because of the sins of the world. He came to save all sinners that believe in Him. Although no one can fully understand this, He took the sins of all His people upon Himself, and He died in their place.

Before He died He said "Father, forgive them, for they do not know what they are doing". He was talking about the Jews[8] as they were the people who wanted Him dead. But even as He was dying He gave them another chance. He forgave them for what they had done and decided that they should have another opportunity to believe in Him.

And so the Lord Jesus died. He was taken down from the cross, and wrapped in linen and laid in a tomb with a large stone rolled in front of it.

The Resurrection

Three days later some women went to the tomb and saw that the stone had been rolled aside. They looked inside and the body of the Lord Jesus had gone. They turned around and saw two angels. These angels told the women that the Lord Jesus had been raised from the dead, and was alive again. Now He would be alive for evermore. As the Lord Jesus is God we know He will be alive for ever - and so He is alive today.

The women were reminded by the two angels that the Lord Jesus said He would rise from the dead on the third day. He had told the disciples this, but they had not understood and had not believed Him. Immediately, the women went to tell the others that Jesus had risen from the dead and was alive. At first, they did not believe it, but later they did. Then the Lord Jesus began to appear to many different people at different times.

However, although He still looked human, He could appear and disappear when He liked. Some days He appeared to the eleven disciples and taught them many wonderful things. He opened their understanding of all that was written about Him by the prophets, and by Moses. They began to understand all about God's great plan and purpose, and at last they became great teachers for God.

The Ascension

Then, one day, after having taught the eleven disciples many things the Lord Jesus ascended into heaven out of sight, and that was the last time He was seen on earth. Before He went He said that one-day He would return to earth. This will happen some time in the future, and then He will set up His wonderful Kingdom, and reign over the earth as King.

As He had forgiven the Jews while He was on the cross, the eleven had the task of trying to get the Jews to repent of their sin of rejecting Jesus and turn back to God. Because the Lord Jesus had taught the eleven perfectly, they became very good teachers, and began to do what He had asked them to do. He left the eleven disciples and all the other believers to carry on His teaching. Some of the leading disciples were also known as apostles. A disciple is a learner. An apostle is someone who is sent on a mission. So the eleven disciples were apostles to the people of Israel.

****

Map of Jerusalem

The suggested plan of the City of Jerusalem below also shows possible locations for the main events in this chapter.

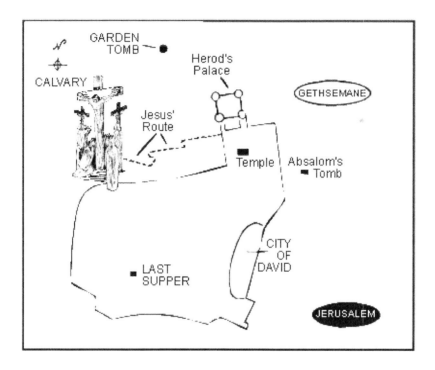

The Lord Jesus goes back to Heaven

Questions

1. Why did Jesus die on the cross?
2. What happened three days later?
3. What happened a little while after that?
4. Where is the Lord Jesus today?
5. What is a disciple?
6. What is an apostle?

Main References

Luke	22:15	The Passover
	22:34	The prophecy that Peter will deny knowing Jesus
	22:47-48	Judas betrays the Lord Jesus
	22:56-62	Peter denies the Lord Jesus three times
	22:70	The Lord Jesus states clearly that He is the Son of God and in so doing claims equality with God (see John 5:18 and 10:33)
	23:20	Pilate wants to let the Lord Jesus go
	23:33	The Lord Jesus is crucified
	23:34 forgiven	The Lord Jesus prays for the Jews to be
	23:53	The Lord Jesus is laid in the tomb
	24:6	The angels tell the women the Lord Jesus is alive again
	24:44-45	The Lord Jesus opens the understanding of the disciples
	24:51	The ascension of the Lord Jesus
Acts	1:9	The ascension of the Lord Jesus
	1:11	The promise that the Lord Jesus will return to earth (see also John 14:3 and elsewhere)

Please read now, or after you have read this book:

Luke 22, 23 & 24; and Acts 1.

God's Plan so far

Jesus is born in Bethlehem:
The dove from heaven; Miracles
Forgiving sins and eternal life
The Jews turn away: Parables
The Transfiguration
Judas and Satan
Pilate - the Roman Governor
The death of the Lord Jesus
 The Lord Jesus is alive again
The Lord Jesus ascended to heaven

13. Peter and the Apostles

(Acts 1-9)

We have heard how the eleven disciples were left on earth to be apostles, to spread the news of the Lord Jesus to all the people of Israel. The Lord Jesus had asked His Father to forgive the people of Israel when He was dying on the cross and so they had been given another opportunity to believe in the Lord Jesus.

One of the first things the eleven apostles did was to choose another apostle to take the place of Judas Iscariot, the one who had betrayed the Lord Jesus to the authorities. When the Jews had important decisions to make, God had told them to cast lots. In this way God guided their decision-making. So the apostles chose two men, Joseph Barsabbas and Matthias, and cast lots to decide which would be the twelfth apostle. The lot fell on Matthias, and so he joined the other eleven.

The Holy Spirit

To help the apostles do their work they were given God's Holy Spirit. This happened on one of the Jews' special feast days called Pentecost. The twelve apostles, and all the other believers in Jerusalem, were sitting in a house together when a violent wind came from heaven and filled the whole house. Then they saw what seemed to be like tongues of fire resting on each of their heads. After this they were all filled with the Holy Spirit and began to speak in other languages.

A great crowd of people gathered outside the house when they heard the noise, and they were amazed when they all heard people speaking to them in their own language. Then Peter stood up and spoke to the crowd. He explained that God had filled them with His Holy Spirit. He also explained that Jesus, the one whom they had crucified, was truly their Lord, and the Christ, their Messiah. After this, three thousand people in the crowd became believers in the Lord Jesus.

Now that they were full of the Holy Spirit the apostles could do many wonderful things. They began to perform miracles of healing, just like the Lord Jesus had done when He was on earth. These miracles were signs to the Jews that God was working with the apostles, giving the Jews yet another chance to repent and accept Jesus as their God, their Saviour and their King.

Soon after being filled with the Holy Spirit, Peter and John went to the temple to pray one afternoon. A man who was crippled from birth lay by the gate to the temple. He used to beg for money from the people going in and out. When he saw Peter and John, he asked them for some money too. But Peter told him he had none to give. Instead he took the man by the hand, lifted him up, and said to him, "In the name of Jesus of Nazareth, walk." The man jumped up, and started walking and leaping and praising God.

Many people gathered around, amazed at this miracle. Again, Peter spoke to the crowd. He told them that Jesus was the one whom the prophets had spoken about. He was the Christ. He told them that if they repented and accepted Him as their Saviour, He would return to earth, then and there, and He would be their Messiah and set up His kingdom. Again, many more people believed, and put their faith in the Lord Jesus. The number of men who believed was about five thousand.

Opposition

However, the leaders of the people, the rulers, the elders and the teachers did not believe that Jesus was the Christ. They did not believe that Jesus could raise people from the dead. They wanted to stop Peter and John from speaking to the people, so they arrested them and then commanded them to stop teaching in the name of Jesus. But Peter and John replied that they could not help talking about all they had seen and heard. The leaders and elders could not decide how to punish them, especially as so many people were praising God for the wonderful miracle they had done. So the leaders let Peter and John go after making more threats.

The apostles continued to do many such miracles. They were all signs to the Jews that they should repent and believe in Jesus Christ as their Lord and Saviour. If the whole nation, including the leaders, accepted Jesus as their Messiah He would return to them just as He had promised. But the chief priests and elders were hard-hearted, and most of them refused to believe in Jesus, despite all the many signs they saw the apostles performing every day.

One time they arrested the apostles and put them in prison, but they were miraculously set free by an angel of the Lord. God was not going to let men stop His message from being proclaimed. When they were questioned by the High Priest again, Peter and the others replied, "We must obey God rather than men!"

They spoke again of Jesus rising from the dead, but instead of believing, the Jewish rulers refused to listen, and wanted them dead. One of the Pharisees however, whose name was Gamaliel, persuaded them to let the apostles go. He told his fellow rulers that if what Peter and the others were saying was from God, then they would never be able to stop them. Men cannot fight against God he told them, and he was right.

 Soon there were more and more believers. Even many of the priests believed in Jesus. However, as their numbers grew, so did the determination of those against them. One day, a man called Stephen, who was full of faith and the Holy Spirit, was seized and dragged before the ruling council, the Sanhedrin. He spoke of his faith, and ended by saying he saw Jesus standing at the right hand of

God. At this the whole group of people rushed at him, dragged him outside, and stoned him to death. He was the first believer to die for his faith in the Lord Jesus.

Saul of Tarsus

Standing close by while Stephen died, was a young man called Saul who watched what was going on. He approved of all that had happened. He thought all who believed in Jesus should be caught and thrown into prison. Therefore many of the believers were afraid, and left Jerusalem for safer places to live. However, the apostles stayed behind and carried on spreading the news about the Lord Jesus, in spite of the danger they were in.

Later, not content with dragging both men and women from Jerusalem off to prison, Saul asked the high priest to let him go to Damascus and capture believers there as well. He wanted to bring them back to Jerusalem to stand trial. The high priest agreed, and Saul set off.

When he was nearly there, suddenly a light from heaven flashed around him. He fell to the ground and heard a voice say "Saul, Saul, why do you persecute me?" Saul asked, "Who are you, Lord?" The voice replied, "I am Jesus, whom you are persecuting. Now get up and go into the city, and you will be told what you must do."

When Saul got up, he found he could see nothing around him. He had been struck blind. The men who were travelling with him guided him to Damascus where, for three days, Saul remained blind. He did not eat or drink anything.

Then a faithful disciple of the Lord called Ananias was sent to Saul by God. Ananias placed his hands on Saul, and immediately he could see again, and Saul was filled with the Holy Spirit.

From that day on Saul was a believer in the Lord Jesus Christ. He felt so ashamed of himself for persecuting the believers, and thought himself to be the worst of all sinners. He began to preach Christ in the local synagogues in Damascus, and all the Jews who heard him were amazed. They knew he had once persecuted them, but now, instead, there he was, preaching to them and teaching that Jesus was the Christ.

After some time, just as Saul had persecuted the believers, others were eager to capture him, and wanted to put him to death. He was no longer safe in Damascus, so one night some of the believers helped him escape from the city. From there he went to Jerusalem, and met Peter and the other apostles. However, after just a few days his life was in danger there too, so he was sent off to Tarsus, the city where he had been born.

****

Possible routes Paul took from Jerusalem to Damascus

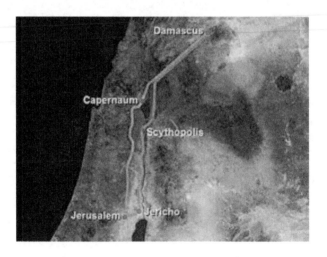

Peter and the Apostles

Questions

1. What did Peter say would happen if the Jews repented and accepted Christ as their Saviour?
2. Who opposed Peter, John and the early Jewish Christians?
3. How did Saul become a believer in the Lord Jesus Christ?

Main references

Acts   1:15-26   Matthias is chosen as the twelfth apostle

2:1-4   The apostles receive the Holy Spirit

3:1-10   Peter and John heal a lame man - an example of the miracles

3:17-21   If the Jews repented, Christ would return

5:17-20   Peter and the apostles put in prison, and freed by an angel

7:54-60   Stephen is stoned

8:1-3   Saul persecutes the church

9:1-6   Saul is converted

9:26-30   Saul returns to Tarsus

Please read now, or after you have read this book:

Acts 1-9

God's Plan so far

Jesus is born in Bethlehem
The dove from heaven
Miracles
Forgiving sins and eternal life
The Transfiguration
Judas and Satan
The death of the Lord Jesus
The Lord Jesus alive again
The Lord Jesus ascended up to heaven
Matthias replaces Judas
The Holy Spirit
Opposition
Saul believes in Jesus

14. Paul and the Gentiles

(Acts 10-28)

Saul was sent to Tarsus for safety, and more than ten years went by before he visited Jerusalem again. Meanwhile, Peter and the apostles continued to spread the news of Jesus Christ to all the Jews in Jerusalem, and in the towns nearby. They continued to do many wonderful miracles which were signs to the Jews that God was working with them. Peter knew that if they all repented, including the leaders and elders in Jerusalem, that Jesus would return to them as He had promised. Then the whole nation of Israel would be saved and they would take God's good news to all the other nations as Abraham had been promised so many years ago.

However, gradually it became clear that many of the Jews were not going to accept Jesus as their Saviour and Messiah. Just as had happened many times in the past, many of them hardened their hearts, and refused to listen to Peter and the others. So God used a final plan with the Jews, and Peter was the first to know about it.

The Gentiles

One day, Peter was praying on the roof of a house in a town called Joppa, when he became very hungry. While he was waiting for a meal to be prepared, he fell into a trance. He saw a large sheet come down from heaven which was full of animals and birds which God had told the people of Israel they must not eat. They were unclean. But a voice came to Peter and told him, "Get up, Peter. Kill and eat." Peter said that he would not because the animals and birds were unclean. Then the voice told him that God had made them clean. This happened three times, and then the sheet was taken up into heaven.

Peter wondered what all this meant. While he was still puzzled, the Holy Spirit told him that three men were looking for him, and that he should go with them, as God had sent them. Sure enough, three men arrived and announced that they were from Cornelius. Cornelius was a Roman centurion and he was a Gentile.

Peter knew that his job was to spread the news to the Jews, rather than to the Gentiles, but as the Holy Spirit had told him to go to Cornelius, he did as he was instructed. When he arrived, he told everyone there that although it was against Jewish custom for a Jew to associate with Gentiles or visit them, God had shown him that nobody should be called unclean.

Cornelius was a righteous and God-fearing man, and wanted to hear Peter's message about Jesus and His resurrection. Peter spoke to him and everyone with him. Peter told them that everyone who believed in Jesus would receive forgiveness of their sins.

While Peter was speaking the Holy Spirit came upon all who were listening to him. The believers who had accompanied Peter there were astonished that the gift of the Holy Spirit had come upon the Gentiles.

This was the final part of God's plan for the Jews. His message was to be given to the Gentiles at the same time as to the Jews. God wanted to provoke the Jews so that when they saw many Gentiles believing in Jesus as their Saviour, that they would realise what they were missing. God wanted the Jews to copy the Gentiles, believe in the Lord Jesus and be saved. Cornelius and the people with him were the first Gentiles to become believers in the Lord Jesus and to be filled with the Holy Spirit. They were the beginning of this final part of God's plan for the people of Israel.

Peter returned to Jerusalem and explained to all the Jewish Christians there what had happened. When they heard that the Holy Spirit had come upon these Gentiles they praised God.

More Gentiles

After this, some Jews who had left Jerusalem after Stephen had been stoned started speaking to Gentiles about the wonderful news of the Lord Jesus. They were in a town called Antioch. When Peter and the others heard about this they sent a man called Barnabas to find out what was happening.

When he got there Barnabas was very pleased to see how many Gentiles believed. Then Barnabas went to Tarsus to look for Saul. When he found him they went to Antioch together. There they met with the believers for a whole year, and taught many people. It was in this town of Antioch that the believers were first called Christians.

Then one day the Holy Spirit spoke to them and said "Set apart for me Barnabas and Saul for the work to which I have called them." They were chosen by God to travel to different nations, spreading the good news of the Lord Jesus. They were to speak first to the Jews in each city they visited and after that to the Gentiles.

From this time on Saul was called Paul, as this was his Roman name, and one which Gentiles were familiar with. Paul became a great man for God. Just as Peter led the Jewish believers in Jerusalem, Paul was recognised as a great leader of both the Jewish and Gentile believers in many different towns and cities throughout the Roman Empire.

To the Jews first

Wherever Paul went, first he spoke to the Jews about the Lord Jesus, and then he spoke to the Gentiles. God used Paul to put this part of His plan into action. God told Paul that He hoped the Jews would copy the Gentiles, and put their faith in the Lord Jesus too.

After his first journey to many different towns and cities, Paul returned to Antioch for a time. While he was there some men visited him and the other Christians. These men said the Gentile Christians should obey the Law of Moses. However, only the Jews, the people of Israel, had been told by God to keep the Law of Moses. The Gentiles had never been told to do so.

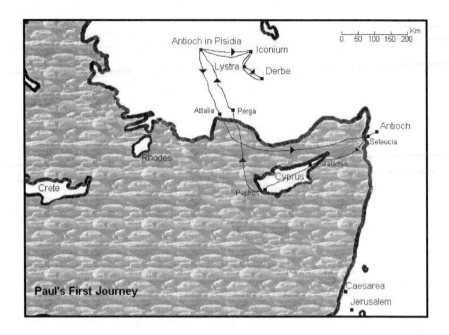

Paul's First Journey

Paul and Barnabas, and some others, went to Jerusalem to discuss this with Peter and the other apostles. They held a big council meeting. In the end the council agreed that the Gentile Christians did not have to keep the Law of Moses. They did however make a list of four things that the Gentile believers should not do. They were all things which the unbelieving Gentiles did in their pagan temples. Christians were never to act like pagan worshippers.

So the council wrote a letter which was sent out to Gentile Christians everywhere explaining that they should keep themselves from doing the four things on the list.

Paul's journeys

After this, Paul spent many more years travelling from place to place. He wrote many letters to the different people he met. In his letters he encouraged them to put their trust in the Lord Jesus, to follow Him, and to act in ways that would please Him.

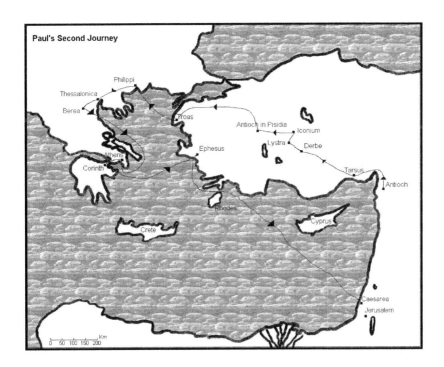

Paul's Second Journey

Like Peter and the other apostles, Paul could also do wonderful miracles through the power of the Holy Spirit. He healed many people, and through these miracles the Jews knew that God was with him.

Like the other apostles, Paul's life was often in great danger. One of the letters he wrote to a group of Christians in Corinth included a long list of all the dangers he had been through in order to spread the good news of the Lord Jesus. He had been in prison, flogged severely, and exposed to death many different times. He had been lashed, beaten with rods, and one time stoned until he was nearly dead. He had been shipwrecked three times and was often cold, hungry and thirsty. He was in danger from rivers, seas, bandits, from Jews and Gentiles in cities and in the country. He had worked himself almost to death for the sake of spreading the wonderful news about Jesus Christ.

After Paul had completed three long journeys, which had taken him many years, he arrived back in Jerusalem once again. There he was arrested and bound in chains by the Romans because so many of the Jews wanted to kill him. Because he was in danger of being killed by a mob of Jews, the Romans took Paul to Caesarea, where he was kept in prison for over two years.

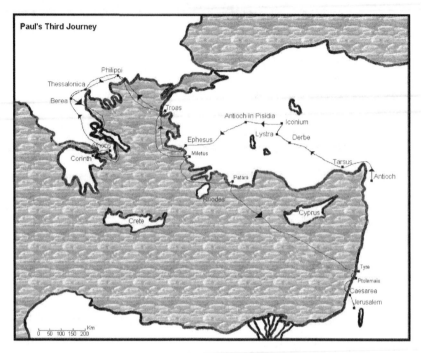

Isaiah's prophecy

After that, Paul asked to go to Rome to have his case decided by Caesar himself - the head of the Roman Empire. After another long and dangerous journey, in which he was shipwrecked, Paul finally arrived in Rome to await his trial.

While he was there he was allowed to live in a house, with a Roman soldier to guard him. When people visited Paul he carried on telling them about Jesus and who He really was. However, although some of the Jews who came to see Paul were convinced that Jesus was their Saviour, many others still refused to believe.

By this time over thirty years had gone by since the Lord Jesus had died. Although many Jews had put their faith in the Lord Jesus, many more had not. Even though God had allowed Gentiles to receive the Holy Spirit this had not provoked the Jews to believe in Jesus and be saved. Instead, many Jews had become hostile towards the Gentile Christians and wanted them dead.

One day, when Paul was speaking to the Jews in Rome, he reminded them of Isaiah's words to them. Isaiah had been one of the prophets sent to the people of Israel hundreds of years before. He had told them that although the nation of Israel would always be told the truth about God, they would refuse to listen and understand. Although it would be quite clear to their eyes, their ears and their hearts, they would still refuse to accept the truth about God and His plan for them.

Isaiah had been told by God that one day Israel would become so blind, deaf and hard-hearted that God would not be able to use them nor would He bless them until a long period of time had passed. Paul told this to the Jewish leaders in Rome and then he said to them, "I want you to know that God's salvation has been sent to the Gentiles, and they will listen."

****

The Letter for the Jerusalem Council

Below is a copy of the letter the Jerusalem Council sent to the Gentiles, telling them to abstain from four things. Can you remember what those four things were? The letter is in Acts 15:23-29.

The apostles and elders, your brothers, To the Gentile believers in Antioch, Syria and Cilicia: Greetings.

We have heard that some went out from us without our authorization and disturbed you, troubling your minds by what they said. So we all agreed to choose some men and send them to you with our dear friends Barnabas and Paul - men who have risked their lives for the name of our Lord Jesus Christ. Therefore we are sending Judas and Silas to confirm by word of mouth what we are writing.

It seemed good to the Holy Spirit and to us not to burden you with anything beyond the following requirements:

You are to abstain

from _____ sacrificed to _____,

from _____,

from the meat of _____ animals

and from _____ immorality.

You will do well to avoid these things.

Farewell.

Isaiah's Prophecy

Here are the words of Isaiah's prophecy. You can find them in Acts 28 28:25-30. Fill in the blanks.

They [The Jews] disagreed among themselves and began to leave after Paul had made this final statement:

"The Holy Spirit spoke the truth to your forefathers when he said through Isaiah the prophet: Go to this people and say,

'You will be ever _____
      but never _____;
you will be ever _____
      but never _____.'
For this people's heart has become calloused;
they hardly _____ with their ears,
and they have _____ their eyes.
Otherwise they might _____ with their eyes,
_____ with their ears,
_____ with their hearts and turn,
and I would _____ them.

Therefore I want you to know that God's salvation has been sent to the _____, and they will listen!"

Paul and the Gentiles

Questions

1. Who was the first Gentile in the Acts of the Apostles to become a believer in the Lord Jesus Christ?
2. When Paul travelled from place to place, who did he give the message to first; Jews or Gentiles?
3. Why was the message sent to the Gentiles at that time?
4. What did Isaiah prophesy would happen to the people of Israel if they refused to believe the message about Christ?

Main References

Galatians	2:1	Saul remains in Tarsus for over ten years
Acts	10:1-48	Peter and the first Gentile convert, Cornelius
Romans	11:11-14	An attempt to make the Jews repent by making them jealous of the Gentiles
Acts	11:26	Disciples first called Christians in Antioch
	13:2	The start of Paul's first journey
	13:42-52	Paul goes first to the Jews, and then to the Gentiles
Romans	1:16	The gospel first to the Jews
	2:9-11	Judgment and blessing, first to the Jews
	3:1-2	The advantages in being a Jew
	9:1-9	The covenants belong to Israel
Acts	15:1-35	The Council at Jerusalem
2 Corin.	12:12	Paul performs many signs, wonders and miracles
2 Corin.	11:23-28	Paul's dangers
Acts	21:27	Paul is arrested
	28:26-28	God's salvation sent directly to the Gentiles.

Please read now, or after you have read this book:

Acts 10-20; Galatians 2; 2 Corinthians 11 & 12; Romans 1-3, 9-11; Acts 21-28.

God's Plan so far

Jesus is born in Bethlehem
The dove from heaven
Miracles and teaching
Forgiving sins and eternal life
The death of the Lord Jesus
The Lord Jesus alive again
The Lord Jesus ascended up to heaven
The Holy Spirit
Opposition
Saul believes in Jesus; Paul and the Gentiles
The Jerusalem Council; To the Jew first
Israel blind, deaf and hard-hearted; Isaiah's prophecy
Israel no longer God's special people
Salvation sent to the Gentiles

15. God's Plan for Today

(Ephesians, Philippians, Colossians, 1 & 2 Timothy, Titus, Philemon)

Paul told the Jews that God's salvation was sent to the Gentiles, and that they would listen. He wrote to many of the different people he had visited over the years. Each group of believers was called a church, and in each of these churches there were both Jews and Gentiles. When he wrote to them from Rome he told them all about the change in God's great plan for them.

No longer were the Jews first. No longer was God going to wait for them to repent and follow Him. No longer was He going to let the Gentiles wait until the people of Israel could spread the message to them. God decided that He would go directly to the Gentiles, without the help of the Jews.

Paul wrote to all the Christians, both the Jews and the Gentiles who believed, to tell them about God's new plan for them. God had kept this plan a secret, and so it had never been known before. It was a wonderful plan. No longer were the Jews to be first, and the Gentiles second to them. Now Jewish and Gentile Christians were equal one with another. There was to be no difference between them any longer.

If either a Jew or a Gentile believed that the Lord Jesus died for their sins, He would save them, forgive them and give them a wonderful gift. This gift was that after they died God would one day raise them from the dead, in the same way that Jesus rose from the dead. They would be given new bodies, like Christ's resurrection body. And they would be righteous, just as Christ is righteous.

Eternal life in the heavenly places

In this new resurrection life they would not be like we are today. They would have a different kind of body called a spiritual body, just like Christ's resurrection body. And they would be perfect - just as Christ is perfect. They would live in *the heavenly places,* which are far above all. This is the place where the Lord Jesus went to when He ascended back into heaven. So everybody who believes in the Lord Jesus and who then dies is just as if he were asleep. One day God will wake up all these believers. Then they will live forever in the heavenly places.

Eternal life on earth

Before, God's plan for the Jews had been a different one. God had promised the Jews a land of their own, and the wonderful gift that He had promised them was that after they died, they would live again on a perfect earth[9]. We know God never breaks a promise so this too will happen one day. All the Jews who believed in God and followed Him, and then died before God's plan changed, are just as if they are asleep. One day God will wake all of them up and they will live again upon the earth.

Changes in God's plan

After Paul wrote these special letters to the Christians from prison in Rome many things changed. Everyone who believed, whether Jew or Gentile, from that time on, would spend their eternal life in the heavenly places, and not on the earth.

The Law abolished

Also God told those Jews who did believe in Jesus that they no longer had to keep all the Law God gave Moses. There were rites and ceremonies they no longer had to perform; feasts they no longer had to have; festivals they no longer had to observe; and certain days they no longer had to keep. However, God still wanted them to love Him and love others. He still wanted them to live good lives. And it was the same for the Gentiles. God wanted them to love Him and others, and to live good lives too.

Miracles cease

God did not use signs and wonders and miracles with people any more. He had used these with the people of Israel many, many times to show that He was working with them. Moses had used them in Egypt and in the wilderness. The Lord Jesus had used them and so had Peter and the apostles. Then finally, Paul had used them. However, none of these miracles had ever had any lasting effect.

In spite of all the miraculous signs the people of Israel had seen Moses perform, they still did not remain faithful to God. And all the miracles Jesus performed did not stop the Jews rejecting Him and crucifying Him. And all the miracles performed by Peter and Paul and the apostles did not cause the Jews to turn and repent and believe in Jesus as their Lord and Saviour.

God wanted the Gentiles to have faith in Him without them seeing miracles and signs. God had never sent many miracles and signs to the Gentiles in the past, and He did not change this.

So today, we can put our faith in the Lord Jesus without seeing any of the wonderful miracles which happened many years ago. All we have to do is believe in the Lord Jesus, and He will forgive us our sins and grant us eternal life. After we have died, one day we will be raised to life again, just like Jesus rose from the dead.

We know this because of what is written in the Bible. The Bible is the Word of God, written by many different people. Moses, the prophets, Peter, Paul and many others wrote down what God told them. God gave us the Bible so that we can read about Him and learn more about Him. All the stories we have heard are in the Bible, but there are also many others. It is a wonderful book. The Bible also tells us what will happen in the future, although this part is difficult to understand.

****

Ephesians 2:4-7

Fill in the missing words of these important verses.

But because of his great _____ for us, God, who is _____ in mercy, made us _____ with Christ even when we were dead in transgressions - it is by _____ you have been saved. And God raised us up with Christ and _____ us with him in the _____ _____ in Christ Jesus, in order that in the _____ ages he might show the incomparable _____ of his grace, expressed in his _____ to us in Christ Jesus.

God's Plan for Today

Questions

1. What do we have to do to receive the gift of eternal life?
2. Where will we spend our eternal life?
3. Do we have to obey all the laws that God gave to Moses, today?
4. If not, why not?

Main References

Ephesians	1:18-21	The heavenly places
	2:4-8	The heavenly places
	2:14-15	The Law abolished for Jewish Christians
	2:13-18	Jewish and Gentile Christians become one
	3:1-5	God's secret new plan not known before
	3:6	Jewish and Gentile Christians become one
	3:8-9	God's secret new plan not known before
Colossians	1:25-27	God's secret new plan not known before
	2:13-17	The Law abolished for Jewish Christians
Philippians	2:25-27	Paul could not heal Epaphroditus
	3:21	New resurrection bodies, like Christ's
1 Timothy	5:23	Paul could not heal Timothy
2 Timothy	4:20	Paul did not heal Trophimus

Please read now, or after you have read this book:

Ephesians 1-3; Colossians 1-2; Philippians 2-3; 1 Timothy 5; 2 Timothy 4.

God's Plan so far

Jesus is born in Bethlehem
Miracles and teaching
Forgiving sins and eternal life
Crucifixion, Resurrection, Ascension
The Holy Spirit
Peter and the Jews; Paul and the Gentiles
To the Jew first
Israel become blind, deaf and hard-hearted
Israel no longer God's special people
The Law abolished
Miraculous signs ceased
Salvation sent to the Gentiles
God's new secret plan
All believers equal
The heavenly places

16. God's Plan for the Future

(Revelation and other prophetic writings)

Some time in the future Christ will return to earth, just as He promised many years ago. Before this happens, the Bible tells us about several events which will take place first. One of these will be the rebuilding of the Jewish temple in Jerusalem. This was completely destroyed by the Romans not long after Paul had written to the Christians telling them of the change in God's plan. The Jews have always wanted to rebuild the temple, and one day they will.

An important and powerful man will make an agreement with the Jews that they can rebuild their temple. He will guarantee that they can have their sacrifices in their temple for seven years. However, just as Judas allowed Satan to influence him, so this man will follow Satan as well.

For three and a half years there will be peace in Israel and the Jews will build their temple and start their sacrifices. However, after three and a half years Satan will appear on the scene. He and the wicked angels which follow him will be thrown out of heaven by Michael and the good angels. They will come down to earth and make sure that the seven-year agreement is broken. Satan will persecute all the Jews living in and around Jerusalem. They will escape to the wilderness and be protected by God for the next three and a half years until Christ returns. Meanwhile, Satan will give great power to the man who made the agreement with the Jews.

False miracles

This man will receive a deadly wound, but he will be miraculously healed. The people who see this will be astonished, and worship him. They will also worship Satan who gave this man his power. This man will be the most evil person who has ever lived on earth and become a powerful and wicked leader.

Then another man will arise and he will be a false prophet. He will set up an image of the wicked leader in the holiest place of the temple of God in Jerusalem. This prophet will be so powerful, he will be able to make the image itself speak. He will even be able to bring fire down from heaven, a miracle which will convince some of the Jews that this false prophet is really from God. He will tell the Jews to worship the image of the wicked leader which is set up in the temple. This will force the Jews to break the first commandment which says that the Jews should worship no-one but the one, true God. But the wicked leader will order all the Jews who refuse to worship his image in their temple to be killed.

He will also force all the Jews to receive a mark on their right hand or forehead. This mark will be a number which represents the name of the wicked leader. This number is 666.

For three and a half years, this wicked leader will have absolute authority, and Satan will be worshipped, as he always wanted from the very beginning.

God's provision

During this time, the Jews who escaped to the wilderness will be fed and protected by God. Also, God will not leave the Jews in Jerusalem and the land around without any witness of Himself. He will send two prophets to speak to everyone. They will have great power given to them by God.

They will be able to stop it raining, to turn water into blood and to strike the earth with plagues as often as they want. They will have the same power given to them that God gave Moses when he led the people of Israel out of Egypt.

But after about three and a half years, when the time for their witness is over, God will allow them to be killed. All the unbelievers will rejoice - those that worship Satan and his man. But then God will raise the two witnesses back to life and they will ascend into heaven to be with God.

Christ's return

Finally, seven years after the agreement to rebuild the temple, Christ will return to the earth, just as He said He would when He ascended into heaven many years ago. When He comes, He will save the Jewish people from Satan and the wicked leader. Then at last, all the Jewish people will accept Jesus as their Messiah, their Saviour and their King. The wicked leader and the false prophet will be destroyed by God.

Satan will be taken by one of God's angels and locked away for one thousand years and so will all the other wicked angels who helped him. Then Satan will not be able to lead anyone away from God for this period of time. This one thousand years of peace on earth is known as the millennium. It is when God's kingdom comes upon earth.

The day when Christ returns will be a great day of resurrection. All believers will be raised from the dead. Some will have eternal life in the heavenly places, and others will have eternal life on the earth. Those on the earth will go and tell everyone in all the other nations about the Lord Jesus Christ.

The earth will be free from the wickedness of Satan, and people will no longer be deceived by him. They will be able to choose to do the right thing without Satan persuading them to do the opposite. So will be fulfilled God's original plan for the people of Israel to go out to all the nations and convert them. This will be the time when God's kingdom comes upon the earth, when His will is to be done on earth as well as in heaven. It will be the happiest time this world will ever know.

The end of all sin and evil

After the thousand years are over, God will finally destroy Satan and all his wicked angels, just as He had told Satan He would many years before in the Garden of Eden. Satan will then no longer exist[10].

Then there will be a final day of resurrection. This final day is called the day of judgement. On this day God will raise to life everyone else who has ever lived on earth. These are the people who were not raised from the dead the day Christ returned.

God will judge all of them according to what they did while they were on earth. Those whose names are not written in God's book of life, those who rejected God while they were living, will be destroyed forever.

The new creation

Then God will create a new heaven and a new earth and everyone in heaven and everyone on earth will be perfect. No one will ever die. No one will ever do wrong, and there will be no more sin, no more sadness, and no more sorrow. Everyone will love God and everyone will love one another. At last God will have what He always wanted. Everyone will be perfect, just like He is. There will be no illness, no pain, no sorrows and no disappointments. It will be wonderful, and it will last forever.

Conclusion

This is the end of God's great plan. In the beginning God was all alone. Then He made the angels and afterwards He made man. Some of the angels and every man disobeyed God. So God made a plan to lead everyone back to perfection again. He came to earth as a man and took the name Jesus. He died for our sins, so that one day in the future everyone who believes in Him will live again and be perfect like Him.

What is the best thing that we can do? It is to believe in the Lord Jesus Christ. It is to believe that He died for our sins and that through Him we will have eternal life.

****

John 3:16
Fill in the missing words

For God so loved the world that he gave his one and only Son,

that whoever _____ in him shall not

_____ but have

_____ _____.

God's Plan for the Future

Questions

1. What will the Jews do in Jerusalem about seven years before Christ returns?
2. Where will we go, when we are raised from the dead by Christ when He returns?
3. What will the new heavens and the new earth be like?
4. What four things will be missing from the new heavens and new earth? (Revelation 21:1-4)

Main references

Revelation	12:7-17	Satan thrown out of heaven and tries to kill the Jews
	13:1-18	The wicked leader (beast) and the false prophet
	11:3-12	The two prophets sent by God
1 Thessal.	4:13-17	Christ returns; some of the dead raised.
Matthew	24:15-31	The Lord Jesus returns to the earth
Revelation	19:17-21	The wicked leader (beast) and false prophet are destroyed
	20:1-3	Satan is locked away for a thousand years
	20:4-6	The first resurrection
	20:7-10	Satan destroyed
	20:12-15	The last resurrection; unbelievers, death and Hades (hell) destroyed
	21:1-4	God creates new heavens and a new earth

Please read now, or after you have read this book:

Matthew 24; 1 Thessalonians 4; 2 Thessalonians 2; Revelation 11-13 & 20-21.

God's Plan so far

The life of Christ
Crucifixion, Resurrection, Ascension
Israel no longer God's special people
Salvation sent to the Gentiles
God new secret plan; all believers equal
The heavenly places
The Law abolished; Miracles ceased
The temple rebuilt
The wicked man
Satan thrown to earth
Christ returns, some of the dead raised
Satan bound for 1,000 years
The millennium
Satan destroyed
The rest of the dead raised
God creates new heavens and a new earth

More on the Plan of God

Two easy-to-read books going into this subject in a little more detail. If you have enjoyed reading this book, you will find great value in the following two.

Our place in the Plan of God
Brian Sherring

Brian Sherring does an excellent job in outlining the plan and purpose of God as it is revealed in the Bible. He asserts that the Bible assures us that God has a plan and a purpose for the heavens and the earth. It is centred in Jesus Christ and God will reach the goal that he has set.

God's Amazing Plan
David Groves

What had started so wonderfully well appeared to end so disastrously. So we ask …

- Why didn't the Jews respond to Jesus as their Messiah?
- Why did they fail to recognise Him as their king?
- Why did they crucify Him?
- Why did they not know what they were doing?
- Did Jesus get it wrong?

To answer such questions as these and to understand *God's Amazing Plan*, we need to go back in time and seek to understand just what the Jews expected of their Messiah when He came.

****

These books are available as eBooks from Amazon and Apple and as paperbacks from Amazon.

Appendix 1:
An Overview of the
Books of Bible

Part 1: The Books of the Old Testament

The Law
> Genesis
> Exodus
> Leviticus
> Numbers
> Deuteronomy

History
> Joshua, Judges, Ruth
> 1 & 2 Samuel
> 1 & 2 Kings
> 1 & 2 Chronicles

Wisdom
> Job
> Psalms, Proverbs
> Ecclesiastes, Song of Solomon
> Ezra, Nehemiah. Esther

Major Prophets
> Isaiah
> Jeremiah, Lamentations
> Ezekiel
> Daniel

Minor Prophets
> Hosea, Joel, Amos, Obadiah
> Jonah, Micah, Nahum, Habakkuk
> Zephaniah, Haggai, Zechariah, Malachi

Part 2: The Books of the New Testament

The Gospels

Matthew
Mark
Luke
John

Written during the Acts Period

Luke	–	The Acts of the Apostles
Paul	–	Galatians, 1 & 2 Thessalonians, Hebrews, 1 & 2 Corinthians, Romans
James	–	James
Peter	–	1 & 2 Peter
John	–	1 & 2 & 3 John, Revelation
Jude	–	Jude

Written after the Acts Period

Paul	–	Ephesians, Colossians, Philemon, Philippians Titus, 1 Timothy, 2 Timothy

Appendix 2: Summary of the Events in Bible

Part 1: The Old Testament

God
Adam and Eve
Cain and Abel
Noah and the Flood
The Tower of Babel
Abraham, Isaac, Jacob
The Twelve Sons
Joseph taken into Egypt
Slaves in Egypt
Moses and The Plagues of Egypt
The Passover
Escape from Egypt
Crossing of the Red Sea
The Ten Commandments and the Law
Forty Years in the Wilderness

Joshua
The Promised Land
Judges
Kings
Saul, David, Solomon

Civil War in Israel: the Division of the Kingdom
    Northern Kingdom of Ten tribes
        Various Kings &Various Prophets
        Assyrian Captivity
    Southern Kingdom of Two tribes
        Various Kings & Various Prophets
        Babylonian Captivity
Return to Jerusalem

Part 2: The New Testament

The Gospel Period
The Lord Jesus born in Bethlehem
Shepherds and Wise Men
John the Baptist
Satan and the Temptations in the Wilderness
Peter and the Twelve Apostles
The Teachings and Miracles of the Lord Jesus Christ
The Jews do not believe; Parables
The Transfiguration
Judas and Satan
Peter denies knowing the Lord
Trials before the Jewish Council, Pilate and Herod
The Death and Resurrection of Jesus
The Ascension

Acts and Afterwards
The Holy Spirit and Miracles
Peter goes to the Jews
The Jews as a nation do not believe.
Paul goes to some Gentiles
The Jews as a nation still do not believe
God turns away from the Jews as His special nation
Miracles stop
God turns directly to Gentiles; Paul – the new leader
God's New Plan
Believers to have eternal life in the heavenlies

The Future
The Lord Jesus returns to the earth
Satan bound for 1,000 years
Believing Jews raised to have eternal life on a perfect earth
Satan destroyed
New Heavens and New Earth created
Everything is Perfect; God is All in All

Appendix 3: Readings from the Bible

At the end of each chapter in this book we suggested people read certain chapters of the Bible. Below is the title of each chapter of this book, followed by the readings we suggested. You can read a chapter or two a day.

You may also care to obtain copy of the book *Approaching the Bible*, which is published by the Open Bible Trust (www.obt.org.uk). This book is an introduction into studying the Bible. It is simply and clearly written.

1. Adam and Eve in the Garden of Eden
Genesis	1	2
Ezekiel	28:11-19	
Genesis	3	

2. Noah and the Flood
Genesis	4	5	6	7	8	9

3. The Tower of Babel and God's New Plan
Genesis	10	11	12	13	14	15

4. Abraham, Isaac and Jacob
Genesis	16	17	18	19	20	21	22	23	24
	25	26	27	28	29	30	31	32	33
	34	35	36						

5. Joseph in the Land of Egypt
Genesis	37	38	39	40	41	42	43	44	45
	46	47	48	49	50				

6. Moses leads the People of Israel out of Egypt
Exodus	1	2	3	4	5	6	7	8	9
	10	11	12	13	14	15			

7. From the Wilderness to the Promised Land

Exodus	16	17	18	19	20	21	22	23	24
	25	26	27	28	29	30	31	32	33
	34	35	36	37	38	39	40		
Leviticus	23								
Numbers	13	14							
Deuteronomy	28	34							
Joshua	1	2	3	4	5	6			

8. Judges, Kings and Prophets

Judges	1	2	3	4	5	6	7	8	9
	10	11	12	13	14	15	16	17	18
	19	20	21						
1 Samuel	1	2	3	8	9	10			
2 Samuel	5	12							
1 Kings	3								
Isaiah	6	9	35	53					
Micah	5								

9. The Lord Jesus is born

Matthew	1	2
Luke	1	2

10. The Miracles of the Lord Jesus

Luke	3	4	
John	2		
Luke	5	6	7

11. The Lord Jesus is rejected

Matthew	14	15	
Luke	7	8	9
John	6	7	

12. The Lord Jesus goes back to Heaven

Luke	22	23	24
Acts	1		

13. Peter and the Apostles

Acts	2	3	4	5	6	7	8	9

14. Paul and the Gentiles

Acts	10	11	12	13	14	15	16	17	18
	19	20							
Galatians	2								
2 Corinthians	11	12							
Romans	1	2	3	9	10	11			
Acts	21	22	23	24	25	26	27	28	

15. God's Plan for Today

Ephesians	1	2	3	4	5	6
Colossians	1	2	3	4		
Philemon	1					
Philippians	1	2	3	4		
Titus	1	2	3			
1 Timothy	1	2	3	4	5	6
2 Timothy	1	2	3	4		

16. God's Plan for the Future

Matthew	24				
1 Thessalonians	4				
2 Thessalonians	2				
Revelation	11	12	13	20	21

About the Author: Sylvia Penny

Sylvia Penny was born in Bexleyheath, Kent, in 1956. She was educated at Basingstoke High School and Queen Mary's College, before studying accountancy at Oxford Polytechnic. She qualified as a Chartered Accountant and practised in the profession for a number of years, until she went to live in the USA with her husband and was a pastor's wife, taking an active role in the church. On returning to Britain she went back to the accountancy profession and now works part time as an accountant.

Other publications by Sylvia Penny include the book *Salvation: Safe and Secure* and *Satan through the Bible.* She also collated and edited *Woman to Woman,* a collection of articles for women by women and which has received a number of good reviews. An ideal book for women's ministry.

She has also written a number of booklets including *Arminianism or Calvinism?, The Seven Deadly Sins, Loving your Enemies, Lying, Forgiveness, Theories of Creation, Noah's Flood* and *Resurrection: When?* (written with her husband Michael Penny).

Details of these and other publications can be seen on

www.obt.org.uk

They can be ordered from that website but
they are also available as eBooks from Amazon and Apple
and as paperbacks from Amazon.

Further reading:
Books by Sylvia Penny

Woman to Woman
Sylvia Penny

Review 1
Reviewed by Jean Macgregor in
Evangelicals Now

Christian women from all walks of life often
have many plates to spin at once—managing
homes, families, jobs and church activities all
at the same time, with little time left over for themselves or the Lord. This
book could be kept to hand for use in precious moments of quiet
reflection as time allows—and enjoyed.

It is a compilation of 60 articles which first appeared in a magazine called
Search, and are now published in one volume. Each one is short and
interesting, and directed towards all women and their needs.

There are eight sections with headings such as Women in Scripture,
Christian living, Husbands and wives, Raising children, A Christian
perspective on modern-day issues, and the apostle Paul and women. Most
of the articles have Scripture references and could be used as a focus for
a personal quiet time, the basis for a group discussion or as a thought-
provoker while vacuuming around the house

The book is nicely presented and would make a very acceptable gift.

Review 2
Reviewed by Rita Dollar in *Prophecy Today*

A collection of articles by numerous writers on a wide variety of topics,
it is both interesting and helpful. Women will appreciate the scriptural
advice given on day-to-day issues. Husbands and wives, raising
children, financial aspects, gender concerns are all dealt with in a
sympathetic manner.

Thoughtful research has been added to the subjects of Old and New Testament women and how the Apostle Paul addressed women in fledgling churches.

I enjoyed the book. It is a good resource and easily dipped into.

****

Salvation
Safe and Secure?
Sylvia Penny

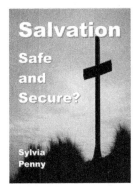

This important book is a thorough treatment of the subject of salvation, asking such questions as …

- What is it, exactly, that saves us?
- Is salvation secure?
- Can it be lost?
- What is 'conditional security'?

It deals with a wide number of issues such as …

- Salvation and works
- The doctrine of rewards
- Lordship salvation
- Free grace theology
- Assurance of salvation
- Why people lose their faith

****

Details of these books and other publications can be seen on

www.obt.org.uk

They can be ordered from that website but
they are also available as eBooks from Amazon and Apple
and as paperbacks from Amazon.

About the Author:
Michael Penny

Michael Penny was born in Ebbw Vale, Gwent, Wales in 1943. He read Mathematics at the University of Reading, before teaching for twelve years and becoming the Director of Mathematics and Business Studies at Queen Mary's College Basingstoke in Hampshire, England. In 1978 he entered Christian publishing, and in 1984 became the administrator of the Open Bible Trust.

He held this position for seven years, before moving to the USA and becoming pastor of Grace Church in New Berlin, Wisconsin. He returned to Britain in 1999, and is at present the Administrator and Editor of The Open Bible Trust. In 2010 he was elected Chair of Churches Together in Reading, and in 2019 Chair of Churches Together in Berkshire, where he speaks in a number of churches. He is one of the chaplains at Reading College and is lead chaplain for all Activate Learning colleges. He is also on the Advisory Committee of Reading University Christian Union.

He lives near Reading with his wife and has appeared on BBC Radio Berkshire and Premier Radio a number of times. He has made several speaking tours of America, Canada, Australia, New Zealand and the Netherlands, as well as ones to South Africa and the Philippines. Some of his many writings have been translated into German and Russian.

In 2019 he was nominated by the Bishop of reading to receive Maundy Money from the Queen for his services to society, the church and Christianity.

As well as writing articles for *Search* magazine and many Bible study booklets, he has also written several major books including: *The Manual on the Gospel of John; 40 Problem Passages; Approaching the Bible; Galatians - Interpretation and Application; The Miracles of the Apostles; Introducing God's Word* (with Carol Brown and Lynn Mrotek); *Introducing God's Plan* (with Sylvia Penny).

More recent books include *The Bible! Myth or Message?* and *The Balanced Christian Life* (based on Ephesians, and is designed for use with Lent Studies and House Group Bible Studies).

His latest books are

- *Paul: A Missionary of Genius*
- *Peter: His life and letters*
- *John: His life, death and writings*
- *James: His life and letter*
- *Joel's Prophecy: Past and Future*
- *Following Philippians*, which he wrote with William Henry and which is ideal for Post-Alpha groups.
- *The Will of God: Past and Present*, which was also written with William Henry.
- *Abraham and his seed*, which he wrote with W M Henry and Sylvia Penny

Details of these books, and other writings, can be seen at

www.obt.org.uk

They can be ordered from that website but
they are also available as eBooks from Amazon and Apple
and as paperbacks from Amazon.

Michael Penny is editor of *Search* magazine
and Sylvia Penny is a frequent contributor.

For a free sample of the Open Bible Trust's magazine *Search*,
please email
admin@obt.org.uk
or visit
www.obt.org.uk/search

End Notes

[1] **Genesis 3:15 - Satan will one day die.**

(1) "He will crush your head" (*NIV*), "It shall bruise thy head" (*KJV*); this figure, expressing fatality, refers to the destruction of Satan. "You will strike his heel" (*NIV*), "Thou shalt bruise His heel" (*KJV*): this figure, not expressing *fatality*, refers to the Lord Jesus Christ. It refers to the suffering He had to undergo on the cross in order to redeem mankind from sin and death, introduced into this world by Satan.

(2) Ezekiel 28:12-19 is a prophecy against a being that was in Eden and is generally accepted to be referring to Satan. Verses 18-19 describe his *destruction*.

(3) Note Hebrews 2:14 where Christ is to "*destroy* him who holds the power of death - that is the devil."

(4) See also *The Companion Bible* note on Genesis 3:15.

[2] **Cain's offering.**

(1) In Genesis 4:3 we see that Cain brought only "fruits of the soil" as an offering to God. In Genesis 4:4 we see that Abel as well as the fruit of the ground, also brought a sheep (note "also" in *KJV*). This sheep was a special sin offering for God to forgive Abel's sins. Thus God was pleased with Abel.

In Genesis 4:7 we read "If you do what is right, will you not be accepted? But if you do not do what is right, sin is crouching at your door." A better rendering of this is "If you do not do what is right, a sin offering is crouching at the door". In other words, even though Cain was a tiller of the ground a sheep had been provided for him so that he, like Abel, should make a sin offering but he refused. Thus God was not pleased with Cain because he refused to accept the sin offering provided.

(2) See J. N. Darby's *New Translation*; Robert Young's *Literal Translation of the Bible*; and E. W. Bullinger's *The Companion Bible* note on Genesis 4:7.

(3) Note also Hebrews 11:4; "Abel offered God a better sacrifice than Cain did."

(4) For a full treatment of this passage, see *The Cain Complex*, in *40 Problem Passages* by Michael Penny.

[3] Genesis 11:4 - The top of the Tower of Babel.

(1) In Genesis 11:4 we read "Come, let us build ourselves a city, with a tower that reaches to the heavens". The words "that reaches" is in italics in the *KJV,* showing that the words are not in the Hebrew but have been supplied by the translators to make sense. A better rendering of the Hebrew is "let us build ourselves a city and a tower whose top is in the heavens" - i.e. whose top is designed like the heavens, with the signs of the Zodiac depicted upon it - as in many ancient temples. This tower was then to be used by the people to try to predict future events and this God has always forbidden. Possibly these people wanted to predict when the next flood would be. However, as God had said there would never be another flood, it showed, again, that people refused to believe and trust Him.

(2) See also Young's *Literal Translation of the Bible* of Genesis 11:4 and *The Companion Bible* note on Genesis 11:4.

[4] Abraham's willingness to sacrifice Isaac.

Abraham was willing to sacrifice Isaac because Abraham believed that if he killed Isaac God would raise Isaac from the dead. This is what we are told in Hebrews 11:17-19: "By faith Abraham, when God tested him, offered Isaac as a sacrifice. He who had received the promises was about to sacrifice his one and only son, even though God had said to him, 'It is through Isaac that your offspring will be reckoned.' *Abraham reasoned that God could raise the dead,* and figuratively speaking, he did receive Isaac back from death."

⁵ To be saved from sin and death.

The consequence and result of sin is death (Romans 6:23). When we are saved from our sins we are forgiven by God and He does not impose the penalty of permanent death - i.e. we do not perish (John 3:16). He gives us the promise of eternal life. He also promises us that in eternal life we shall be righteous, perfect, like He is (2 Corinthians 5:21; Ephesians 5:25-27; Colossians 1:22). So when we are "saved from sin and death" we know that our sins are forgiven and that we shall have eternal life, and will be perfect. This is because in dying for our sins Christ paid the penalty for sin, and redeemed us from sin and death (Romans 3:25-26).

⁶ Son of God.

The New Testament, in a number of places, refers to our Lord Jesus Christ as the *Son of God*. We have not used this in the text as we discovered that a number of people today were confused by the title. How could the *Son of God*, be God? That is the perplexing thought that some have. However, we need to appreciate what the words *Son of God* meant to the people of Israel of that time. We see that they clearly understood it to mean that He was God. For example, in John 10:30-33 we read that the Lord Jesus Christ said, "I and the Father are one." Again the Jews picked up stones to stone Him, but Jesus said to them, "I have shown you many miracles from the Father. For which of these do you stone me?" "We are not stoning you for any of these," replied the Jews, "but for blasphemy, because you, a mere man, claim to be God." To the Jews, to call God your Father, to claim to be the *Son of God*, meant you were claiming to be God. See, also, John 5:17-18.

⁷ Parables.

Many people think that the Lord Jesus used parables to illustrate His teaching so that the people would find it *easier* to understand Him. In fact that wasn't always the case. Initially He did not use parables but taught people directly and clearly. However, when the Jews would not believe Him, then He started using parables. This provoked His disciples to ask,

"Why do you speak to the people in parables?" (Matthew 13:10). The Lord's reply in Matthew 13:11-17 makes it clear that He spoke in parables so that the undiscerning Jews who had rejected Him would not understand Him. Only those interested enough would come to Him to find out the meaning of the parable (e.g. see Matthew 13:36). However, on other occasions, for example with the parable of the Good Samaritan, there was no hidden meaning. The meaning of the parable was clear and obvious, but in such parables as these the Lord Jesus used extreme exaggeration which may have confused or overawed His listeners; see Luke 10:25-37.

[8] Luke 23:34 - Christ prays for the Jews to be forgiven.

The words "Father forgive them, for they do not know what they are doing" do not refer to the Roman soldiers, as some suggest. They refer to the Jews. The Bible makes it clear that the blame for Christ's crucifixion lay with the Jews of His day (Matthew 27:24-25; Acts 5:30 and 10:39). However, Christ's prayer was answered. The Jews were forgiven and were given another chance to accept Christ as their Saviour - see chapter 13.

[9] Eternal life! In heaven or on earth?

In Revelation 21:1-2 we read of a new heaven and a new earth, as well as a New Jerusalem, coming down out of heaven to be upon this earth. From what follows, and from elsewhere in the Bible, it is clear that many of God's people will spend their eternal life on earth. However, others will spend their eternal life in the heavenly places (Ephesians 2:6-7).

Without going into too many details, redeemed people in the Old Testament, whether they were Jews or Gentiles, can look forward to eternal life on the new earth. This would also be the case for those who lived and died during the period covered by the Gospels and the Acts of the Apostles. The Lord's Prayer looked forward to the time when God's kingdom is to come and His will is to be done "on earth" (Matthew 6:10). And in Acts

3:19-21, Peter told the Jews to repent, and said that if they did so that Christ would return to earth and restore all things.

However, part of the secret (mystery) which God revealed at the end of the Acts period told people that in this dispensation of grace, believers, whether they are Jewish Christians or Gentile ones, are to spend their eternal life in the heavenly realms (Ephesians 1:13-14; 2:6-9; 4:30).

[10] Revelation 20:10 - "for ever and ever".

(1) "For ever and ever" is the translation of Greek words which mean, literally, "unto the age of the ages". The use of the word "unto" or "until" shows that this expression does not mean "unending".
(2) The devil will be tormented day and night until the age of the ages. That age ends with "the second death" (v 14), when all evil is destroyed, including Satan. The next age, the age of all ages, commences with the "new heavens and new earth wherein dwelleth righteousness (*KJV*)" or "the home of righteousness" (*NIV*) (Relation 21:1; 2 Peter 3:13). In that age there is "no more death or mourning or crying or pain, for the old order of things has passed away" (Revelation 21:4). Even Satan has passed away and we have reached the time when God brings "all things in heaven and on earth together under one head, even Christ" (Ephesians 1:10) and then God will be all and in all (1 Corinthians 15:28). Under such conditions it would be impossible to have Satan or any other evil existing anywhere in God's perfect and righteous creation.
(3) See also note 1 on "Satan will one day die".
(4) For a full treatment of this verse see *Tormented day and night for ever and ever*, in *40 Problem Passages* by Michael Penny **(www.obt.org.uk).**

.

Printed in Great Britain
by Amazon

40590635R00079